UNCHOSEN

The Memoirs of a Philo-Semite

Julie Burchill

This edition first published in 2015

Unbound
4–7 Manchester Street, Marylebone, London, W1U 2AE
www.unbound.co.uk

Typeset by Unbound
Cover design by Mecob

A CIP record for this book is available from the British Library

ISBN 978-1-908717-96-2 (limited edn)
ISBN 978-1-908717-95-5 (trade edn)
ISBN 978-1-78352-103-6 (paperback trade edn)
ISBN 978-1-78352-153-1 (ebook)

Printed and bound in Great Britain

For Karl Henry, chavar veh hevruta tov me'od, and Leyla Sanai, the bravest broad I've ever met – im ahava

Also by Julie Burchill

LETTER FROM UNBOUND

Dear Reader,

The book you are holding came about in a rather different way to most others. It was funded directly by readers through a new website: **Unbound**.

Unbound is the creation of three writers. We started the company because we believed there had to be a better deal for both writers and readers. On the Unbound website, authors share the ideas for the books they want to write directly with readers. If enough of you support the book by pledging for it in advance, we produce a beautifully bound special subscribers' edition and distribute a regular edition and e-book wherever books are sold, in shops and online.

This new way of publishing is actually a very old idea (Samuel Johnson funded his dictionary this way). We're just using the internet to build each writer a network of patrons. Here, at the back of this book, you'll find the names of all the people who made it happen.

Publishing in this way means readers are no longer just passive consumers of the books they buy, and authors are free to write the books they really want. They get a much fairer return too – half the profits their books generate, rather than a tiny percentage of the cover price.

If you're not yet a subscriber, we hope that you'll want to join our publishing revolution and have your name listed in one of our books in the future. To get you started, here is a £5 discount on your first pledge. Just visit unbound.com, make your pledge and type `unchos3n` in the promo code box when you check out.

Thank you for your support,

Dan, Justin and John
Founders, Unbound

Contents

ONE

A SHORT HISTORY OF PHILO-SEMITISM

In the September of 2012, in a *Times* column very appropriately titled 'Beta Male', one Robert Crampton described a series of recurrent nightmares he had. All the usual stuff was there: zombies, nakedness, being on the run from the police for unspecified but heinous crimes.

And at the end, this one: 'Another scenario is that I choose to go everywhere wrapped in an enormous Israeli flag. I am aware that many people I come across are sniggering, and some others are downright hostile, and even my most ardently Zionist friends are embarrassed, and yet I insist on wearing the flag everywhere...'

This made me laugh. What a sap! As an alpha female, this is not my nightmare but rather my dream, and one I have to some extent lived. I have spent my life wrapping myself in the Jewish flag, sometimes metaphorically, sometimes literally. I open my handbag and half a dozen paper ones on toothpicks, fashioned for me by my friend and Modern Hebrew Language classmate Karl, fall out. I look up from writing and see two full-sized ones staring proudly back from my bookcases, framing the Torah.

Occasionally, when very drunk, I will literally wrap one around me and cry like a baby.

(And whenever I look at my Torah, I feel a burning thrill of shame, recalling the night not long after I met Karl when we cut our thumbs, smeared our mixed blood on the title page and he agreed with me that 'Now we're with them, whatever happens. But it's probably best that we don't tell them about this, in case it's blasphemy.' Beat. 'Do they have blasphemy?')

I look across the room and see it on the bunting which hangs around my permanent window shrine to that modern Jewish heroine Amy Winehouse. I look into my heart, and against its calcified black background I see the blue and the white.

*

Israel. ISRAEL! Say it loud and there's music playing – say it soft, and it's almost like praying. How could any word be so beautiful – and still is real? ISREAL! How I laughed, livid with loathing and replete with revulsion, when I read that the half-witted crooner Bobby Gillespie had fashioned MAKE ISREAL HISTORY from a MAKE POVERTY HISTORY poster while at a party with the solemn intent of, yes, making poverty history! a) In my view, it's a real indicator of the whereabouts of the moral compass of the anti-Zionist zealot (in most cases, lost down the back of some long-gone sofa in some rancid student house) that he would downplay and devalue world poverty in his blind hatred of a tiny democratic state and b) he would write it incorrectly. You total, ocean-going, numb-nuts, Gillespie. And you can't spell!

Well, I can. And I'm going to spell out to anyone with the time and/or the inclination to give me a hearing just why I love the Jews so much. Why, in short, I am a philo-Semite.

*

According to Gertrude Himmelfarb's excellent *The People Of The Book: Philosemitism in England From Cromwell To Churchill*, the phrase was actually invented by anti-Semites, in Germany in the 1880s when the highly regarded (and avowedly anti-Semitic) historian Heinrich von Treitschke, in a speech...referred contemptuously to 'the blind philosemitic zeal of the party of progress.' (Once more, on reading this, I was struck by how many German names strike the English eye as looking Jewish, and reflected for the nth time that this was partly what historically got the German goat. One cannot mistake Smith, Jones or Johnson for a Hebrew handle, after all – but Mann, Stein or Schicklgruber, no problem.)

But I first saw the term in a copy of *Rolling Stone* magazine, of all things. It was a long essay, first person, called CONFESSIONS OF A PHILO-SEMITE. I would have been somewhere between O Levels and *NME*, while still kicking my heels in Bristol. Even now, I remember the gist of the essay, and the last line verbatim, even though I haven't set eyes on it in more than thirty years.

This man, the writer, remembered adoring the Jews from afar at his high school. 'Gentile girls were either pretty or clever; if a Jewish girl was one, she was usually the other,' I remember he wrote. Something like that. He had one of those generic American surnames with 'man' on the end which are sometimes Jewish, sometimes German in origin. (See the Getting Of The Hunnish Goat, above.) So on graduating from high school he had seen his chance, seized the day, left his hometown, enrolled in a college with a high percentage of Jewish students and he had...passed.

HE HAD PASSED AS A JEW! I remember shivering with delight and looking around guiltily, almost hugging myself with glee. It had never occurred to me. Could I...at the *NME*? No one knew me there. I looked at myself in the mirror: white skin, green almond-shaped eyes, big nose, dark blonde hair, narrow but pouty mouth and a great big gap between my two front teeth. I seemed (to myself if to none of my philistine schoolmates) to have what Mary McCarthy's Priss Hartshorn – in McCarthy's brilliant novel *The Group*, a teenage favourite of mine – noted about a classmate's baby:

> *There was no doubt that he appeared to be a child marked for a special destiny, as they said of the Jewish people.*

And Jews came in all hues, I knew that now – I had seen Goldie Hawn on the TV in *There's A Girl In My Soup*, and marvelled that she and Peter Sellers were of the same race. I was sitting with my mum one adorably dreary Saturday night watching it when suddenly, in pursuit of Goldie, Peter Sellers stripped off his swinging skinny-rib polo-neck and presented to her, my Snowball-sipping madre and my permanently-sulking self an upper body so covered in coarse black hair that he looked as though he'd been dipped first in tar, then in iron filings and then, as the finishing touch, had had the inner bags from a dozen heavy-duty vacuum cleaners emptied over him.

I seem to remember that Goldie fainted, though naturally due to the highly sexist nature of 60s films it couldn't be because she was absolutely repelled by the prancing ape in front of her – she was meant to be drunk or overcome with lust or something. Ma and I, being made of sterner stuff, merely looked at each other, and though like most teenage girls I would rather have died than admitted that I had anything in common with my sainted mother, a look passed between us which wordlessly expressed all the endless sorrow, astonishment and plain something-nasty-in-the-woodshedness of being a woman in a man's world. A man's world where, due to them having the power and us having to please them, we were expected to spend half our lives beautifying our unacceptable selves while they reserved the right to go around looking like something which would be more at home being chased through the hills and dales of Tibet by a photo-journalist from the *Fortean Times* – and were still considered to be right royal 'catches'. Still, I remember telling myself, if you really want to marry a Jew you probably will encounter body hair at some point. You can do it, hon. Just lie back and think of Israel.

Anyway, I read on, rapt. It was all going SO well for Pretendy Jew Man. He dated all the prettiest/smartest Jewish girls in his year and then he actually MARRIED one. OK, so he was a liar, and denying his blameless Christian parents. He was PASSING! Faint heart never won fair JAP and all that. But the truth has a habit of refusing to be filed away tidily, and PJM eventually got bug-fuck drunk at a family gathering. His intoxication level must have been a hint of what was coming before he even started speaking his piece; the number of Jews who drink excessively is minuscule compared to Gentiles, especially English Gentiles. At the fun-filled lunches which often follow my Hebrew class, our orchidaceous Israeli teacher sits and blinks with dazed good humour at Karl and I, who think nothing of downing a bottle each of Sancerre – while she toys with a mere glass – before staggering across the road to a cocktail bar to down Mai Tais the size of my thighs while yelling 'L'CHAIM!' in our thrillingly 'special' blend of Wales and West Country accents until we eventually get refused alcohol altogether. Bloody anti-Semites.

Anyway, lit up like a menorah and feeling no pain like the IDF, PJM got up and made a proud, tearful speech in which he told his wife and daughter and in-laws how much he loved them and thanked them for loving him. Except, he explained, the him they loved wasn't real. HE WASN'T JEWISH! Cue a whole lot of upset, though it was far more about the lying than the bloodline. And I remember after all this time the last line, so sad and bold and honest – 'My daughter is half-Jewish. The half that isn't is me.'

*

Not all philo-Semites go as far as lying to their nearest and dearest about their racial make-up, of course. Some convert and some are keen just to look on, cheerleading and getting into scraps on Israel's behalf should the need arise, which it often does. Philo-Semites are as wildly disparate as Cicero and Lindsay Lohan, but I can't help noticing that, over the centuries, a disproportionate number of attractive, kind, clever people are drawn to Jews while those who express hostility to them, from Hitler to Hamza, are often as not repulsive freaks. Think of famous anti-Zionists – Vanessa Redgrave, Patricia Highsmith, George Galloway – and what dreary, dysfunctional, po-faced vanity confronts us. When we consider famous Jew-lovers, on the other hand – Marilyn, Ava, Liz, Felicity Kendal, Martha Gellhorn, Martin Luther King, me – what a sumptuous banquet of radiant humanity we look upon. Life's great puzzlement, to me, has always been not 'What do women want?' or 'Who put the bomp?' but why there are apparently more anti-Semites than philo-Semites and the answer I've ended up with, both empirical and circumstantial, is that there are a lot of dumb people in the world, and a lot of them are anti-Semites. True, not all dumb people are anti-Semites, but all anti-Semites are dumb. Whatever way you slice it, that's a whole lot of mob – flaming pitchforks optional.

So how did philo-Semites come to be so few and far between? The situation always makes me think of Stephen King's masterpiece *The Stand*, in which a handful of freaks are left standing after surviving the plague that cuts friends, family and strangers alike down all around them. Anti-Semitism does that – but the brain-dead still walk and talk like the survivors do, so it's not so noticeable. Until they're given certain easy tests – like being given the chance to choose between, say, abolishing worldwide poverty or abolishing the tiny state of Israel.

The first thing a philo-Semite needs to know – like a hermaphrodite, or a child with divorced parents – is a) it's not your fault and b) you're not alone. Those people over there, who look at the lack of sex, money and/or success in their lives and sincerely believe that The Jews took their portion – they're the weirdos. Elsewhere in *The Group*, the father of one of the upper-middle-class WASP graduates of the title expresses his frustration at his daughter's (relatively) poor prospects to another of the girls thus:

> *With all Helena's education, she had elected to play the piano...and teach finger-painting at an experimental school in Cleveland – to a darned lot of kikes' children, from what Mr Davison had heard. Where was the sense in that, he had asked Kay angrily after lunch...Kay suspected that he was angry because Helena had failed to get* magna cum laude, *when a lot of the Jewish girls had.*

Some of us less than brilliant people admire the Jews because they have always added so much to the store of culture, science and general progression in this sometimes ignorant and miserable world of ours. It's the stark, staring breakdown of the Nobel Prize statistics that always gets me. Between 1901 and 2012, there have been 850 winners. Of those, at least 173 have been Jews, ranging across the categories of Literature, Chemistry, Economics, Medicine and Physics. The tiny state of Israel alone, since only 2002, has had six Nobel Prize winners, compared to five each from the vast nations of Russia and Germany. The American Enterprise Institute's political scientist Charles Murray put it thus:

In the first half of the 20th century, despite pervasive and continuing social discrimination against Jews throughout the Western world, despite the retraction of legal rights, and despite the Holocaust, Jews won 14 percent of Nobel Prizes. In the second half of the 20th century, when Nobel Prizes began to be awarded to people from all over the world, that figure rose to 29 percent. So far, in the 21st century, it has been 32 percent.

Yet Jews only make up about 0.2 percent of the world's population. I mean, go figure. So clever – so hated. What's not to love? Sadly, this level of contribution makes other less than brilliant people bitter. A line cut from the film *Funny Girl*, in which that great Jewish tragedienne Barbra Streisand played that great Jewish comedienne Fanny Brice, had Brice bewailing her fame because 'it makes smaller people feel...too small.' These small people, of whom Hitler was the supreme example, eventually become anti-Semites.

But in my opinion, to choose the Jews is to choose life – not just survival, though they do that well too, but also all of the magic that can arise from the simple state of being a human being. It's no coincidence that the favoured drinking toast of the Jews is 'L'chaim!' – 'To life!', as the wedding party sing in *Fiddler On The Roof*.

The most Jew-hating organization in existence, al-Qaeda, famously said after the 2004 Madrid bombings, 'You love life and we love death', but the Hamas leader Ismail Haniya also said, a year before, to an American journalist, 'the Jews love life more than any other people, and they prefer not to die.' With enemies like that, who needs friends?

Nevertheless, a friend of the Jews I remain. But like they used to say back in the old schoolyard, though, there's always one who has to spoil it for everybody else, and this is as true of philo-Semitism as it is of daytrips to Stonehenge. There's the odd voice here and there which pours scorn on devotion to my chosen team, but these are as often as not strange characters such as the Holocaust-denying musician and 'proud self-hating Jew' Gilad Atzmon, or my late mother-in-law Fran Landesman who, when I expressed outrage that she had been barred from tennis clubs in her native America as a young Jewish girl yelled, 'Screw the righteous anger. I just wanted to join!' Rather as Groucho Marx wouldn't want to belong to any club who would have him, certain sad Jews (the type prodded with such righteously vicious glee in Howard Jacobson's *The Finkler Question*) have internalized the loathing which has been poured on them since they first raised their heads above the Biblical parapet, and are liable to react to philo-Semites with confusion and spite.

Such people are both sinister and silly (to paraphrase Christopher Hitchens' summing up of the WE ARE ALL HEZBOLLAH NOW mob) but entirely unimportant in the face of ancient and continuing Jewish achievement, civilization and success. In 2010, the Jewish journalist Anne Karpf wrote in the *Independent*:

> *We live in post-modern times where some of what looks like anti-Semitism isn't, but, conversely, some*

of what doesn't look like anti-Semitism in fact is. Consider the 'philo-Semitism', for instance, of Michael Gove and Julie Burchill ('the Jews are my favourites'; 'Jews do things so well'). Burchill's philo-Semitism is a form of anti-Semitism, I'd suggest, because it bunches all Jews together, as though we were a single, uniform entity. The idea that all Jews are wonderful is little different from all Jews being hateful: in both cases Jews are stripped of individual characteristics, and are nothing except Jewish – a view to which most racists happily subscribe.

The lack of both clarity and charity in this appalling slur makes me think that the writer has swallowed whole that idiotic saying 'It's a thin line between love and hate' – it's not, you know, it's a dirty great abyss. It is bittersweet to be dissed by a Jew in the *Independent* – which appears to me to be almost hysterical in its anti-Israel sentiment – for being a bad person because one admires the Jews. But considering how confused the writer must be, I think I can just about live with it. For I am but a lowly worshipper at the leaping flame of Jewish accomplishment, and the latest in a very long line at that.

*

Before there were philo-Semites, there were the Anglo-Hebraists – those scholars who, quite rightly, recognized the glory of the Old Testament as superior to the rather tepid New Testament. Gertrude Himmelfarb details the case of the lawyer and scholar Sir Henry Finch, who became obsessed with the desirability of the return of the Jews to their ancient homeland, and in 1621 published a book with a title so long that it surely strikes delight into the hearts of word-count-addicts everywhere: *The World's Resurrection or The Calling of the Jews. A Present to Judah and the Children of Israel that Joined with Him, and to Joseph (that Valiant Tribe of Ephraim) and all the House of Israel that Joined With Him.*

By the mid-17th century, an increasing number of people were equally desirous of Jewish return to the country they had been expelled from in 1290 – when writing of the expulsion from England, Churchill called the Jews 'the most formidable and the most remarkable race which has ever appeared in the world', tempering this tough salute with the tenderness of 'this sorrowful, wandering race...the melancholy caravan, now so familiar, must move on' . Cromwell's re-admittance of them made perfect sense; to me, it would be impossible to love the Jews and not loathe monarchy.

How fitting that it should be Oliver Cromwell – the self-styled 'Puritan Moses' – who asked the Jews to come back to Britain. He was the scourge of the Catholics – and it's hard not to conclude that until the rise of Islam, Catholicism truly was the most Jew-hating religion around. He was the scourge of monarchy – and royals are about as far as you can get from Jews, despite the vast numbers of Jewish princesses. Jews, historically, have tended to be born into abuse and social ignominy and gone on to achieve wealth and social prominence; royals tend to take the opposite route.

It's interesting to compare the apparent affection that

the British royal family have for non-democratic Muslim kingdoms as opposed to its avoidance of democratic Israel. Perhaps this affection is not entirely unconnected to admiration – Arab monarchies have things exactly the way that Prince Charles, for one, sometimes seems to wish they still were here. Who could blame him, while sitting in his Islamic garden, for musing on how easier things would have been with That Woman if, in the Muslim manner, he had been able to merely say 'I divorce you' three times and not afterwards been responsible for her expenses!

When the Clown Prince styled himself 'Defender Of Faiths', it seemed pretty clear to me he was sucking up to Islam. (The bloody history and present-day behaviour of which would very much indicate that other religions need protection from it, rather.) But there has been throughout history the occasional monarchy which has been that far braver and more necessary thing – a Defender Of The Jews.

Some went the whole hog, so to speak, and refused to eat pig. The ancient Khazar kingdom, which by serving as a buffer state between Christians and Muslims helped to block the western spread of Islam in Europe, saw Khazar royalty and much of the aristocracy convert to a form of Judaism during the 8th century. Medieval epic poems of the time refer to the Khazar state as 'the Jewish Giant', so respected were the army of this small country – one of the very few tribal societies on the Asian steppe to successfully make the transition from nomadic to urban.

Other monarchs were simply sympathetic, which was welcome, to say the least, during the mass murder of the Jews which became the norm in pre-war and war-time

Europe. Boris, the Tsar of Bulgaria until 1943, stopped the extradition of Bulgaria's 50,000 Jews, defying Hitler face to face during the war by refusing multiple times to deliver his Jewish subjects. They were disenfranchised and herded into ghettos – but they were saved.

King Zog, one of the few 20th-century monarchs neither to be born to be king or have kinghood thrust upon him but rather to have decided he liked the cut of the jib while serving as mere President, might have seemed a figure straight out of Ruritania when he instituted the Zogist salute (flat hand over the heart with palm facing downwards) and made his family princes and princesses. (Though of course all monarchies started with the second action, even the British one, and we don't seem to think that this in any way makes it ridiculous and lacking in authority.) But when he swore an oath on both the Bible and the Qur'an (as a Muslim attempting to unify the country) and abolished Islamic law in Albania, adopting in its place a civil code, he revealed a sensible and civilized side to his character. In 1938, he opened the borders of Albania to Jewish refugees fleeing Nazi Germany.

Considering that so many Muslim movements fought on the side of the Fascists during the War, this was a two-fisted, open-handed act of real humanity.

Closer to home, Princess Alice of Greece – the mother of the Queen of England's consort – was established as one of the Righteous Among The Nations at a ceremony at Yad Vashem in 1994. The solemnity of the occasion caused even Prince Philip to put aside the racially insensitive patter he is renowned for as he recalled how his mother hid a Jewish widow and her two children in her house in Athens after the Fascist invasion of 1941. When the Gestapo came calling, Princess Alice used the thoroughly reasonable excuse of her deafness to explain that she didn't understand their questions. And the Jewish family stayed there safely until the liberation of Greece.

What a shame that this compassion and empathy for a hounded people has not been carried on by the royal family of this country, who seem more inclined to cosy up to some of the worst undemocratic states in the Middle East than tiny, democratic Israel. The miserly roll-call of visiting royals is meagre indeed – Prince Edward in 2007 to meet members of a youth programme affiliated to the Duke of Edinburgh Awards scheme (I bet that put a spring in their step) and in 1995, Princess Margaret made a five-hour visit to the Sea of Galilee during a trip to Jordan. Though considering the crapulous state she was usually in, she probably thought she was in the Lake District. It was also in 1995 that the Prince of Wails prised himself away from talking to the plants in his Islamic Garden ('Grow, you bally plant, or it's off with your head!') to attend the funeral in Jerusalem of Yitzhak Rabin, representing the Queen. (What do you reckon The Firm drew straws for that, and the joker lost?) Even the Queen Mother, so regularly hailed for standing up to Hitler, seemed to believe that Jewishness could be caught by mere contact with an 'afflicted' person when she wrote a letter to the Queen asking her not to send Prince Charles to school at Gordonstoun, founded and run by a Jewish refugee: 'It's always a tricky one with the heir to the throne,' the *Daily Mail* had her saying, and Eton, her preference, 'would solve many difficulties, one being religion.'

I must say, the feeling is mutual – I really don't like it when we're asked to sing 'G-d Save The Queen' at the end of Zionist rallies, so I sing the words to Hatikvah instead. Like on that Radio 4 panel show, *I'm Sorry I Haven't A Clue*, when people have to sing the words to 'Walk On The Wild Side' to the tune of 'Daisy, Daisy' and the like. It gives me a secret thrill of sedition, that i have rejected my own people for the Other. As the I Ching proverb which serves as the epigraph for Gish Jen's brilliant novel *Mona In The Promised Land* – about a teenaged Chinese American girl who becomes a Jew – has it

He dissolves his bond with his group.
Supreme good fortune.
Dispersion leads in turn to accumulation.
This is something that ordinary men do not think of.

Since the first primitive man looked down his ape-like snout at another primitive man, those born into lowly status have aspired to rise to a higher class. Why should it be any stranger to aspire to intelligence than to wealth? Philo-Semites merely aim their affection at a different group than the usual – one far worthier of admiration, being notable for achieving on their own merits against great odds rather than having everything handed to them on a plate just because their long-dead ancestors were particularly lucky and/or brutal.

The traditional ruling-class English distrust of the Jews is based on this – that it takes the immigrants just a couple of generations to make the same sort of sashay up through the social hierarchy that it takes the indigenous a couple of centuries. Jews are very clever and the English ruling class are very stupid, so naturally English Jews have taken from the poshos a bit of the wealth and property that once was theirs, snatched from the peasantry and bequeathed by robber barons long ago.

As well as cropping up among the suspect usuals – Whitehall Mandarins cuddling up to feudal Arab nations and cold-shouldering democratic Israel – ruling-class anti-Semitism can come out in the strangest places, such as the minds of otherwise clever and widely-travelled novelists. Agatha Christie's writing – contrary to dull-minded received wisdom – is actually quite progressive in some ways; the killer in any given situation is often a pillar of the community; doctor, policeman, judge. But if you read the books she wrote before she realized she shouldn't call people names any more (pre-war, or maybe the year when her publishers decided that the next printing of *Ten Little Niggers* should instead be called *And Then There Were None*), you'll find loads of dodgy stuff. There are 'men of Hebraic extraction, sallow men with hooked noses, wearing flamboyant jewelry' and there's 'the long-nosed Mr. Lazarus,' of whom somebody says, 'He's a Jew, of course, but a frightfully decent one.' The essayist Francis Wheen wrote to me: 'You won't find much of that in her post-war novels, but maybe she continued to think that way. Here's C. Hitchens in *Hitch-22*, on his dinner with Dame Agatha: "The anti-Jewish flavour of the talk was not to be ignored or overlooked, or put down to heavy humour or generational prejudice. It was vividly unpleasant and it was bottom-numbingly boring."'

Other racial groups can be dismissed by the toff –

unfairly, naturally – as thick, but proof of the Jew's intelligence is quickly visible in any society lucky enough to receive him. As if that wasn't enough, he has something equally threatening to the toff in the other hand – the one that doesn't hold money. Because it holds his cock. The sexual threat of the Other is more often that not present in racism ('Coming over here, taking our women!'), and the eternal and apparently insatiable willingness of the Englishwoman to transcend the national stereotype of 'prissy miss' in order to copulate with anyone other than a compatriot has always been a joy to behold. We have the highest percentage of mixed race babies born in the Western world, and the sight of a working class young white woman pushing a charming coffee-coloured child in a stroller is one of the more agreeable sights of the modern urban landscape.

Jewish men have always got lucky with Gentile broads, ever since Ruth jumped ship in the Bible. The syndrome of the silver screen shiksa goddess converting in order to win the hand of the Jewish writer/director/producer is the stuff of legend. Thrillingly, Marlene Dietrich was stripped of her German citizenship by the Nazi regime because 'constant contact with Jews has rendered her entirely un-German' – surely the best ever compliment intended as a diss. Other converts include Marilyn Monroe, Carroll 'Baby Doll' Baker, Carolyn 'Morticia' Jones, Norma Shearer, May Britt, Eleanor Parker, Polly Bergen and, of course, Elizabeth Taylor. Just when one thought that Taylor and Richard Burton couldn't be any more gorgeous a couple, the joint biography *Furious Love*, which chronicles their stormy union, carried a description of a quarrel they had over who was 'more Jewish'. Burton had referred to the Welsh as 'the Jews of Britain', a comment on their self-identity as the outsiders of the United Kingdom. (Ernest Jones, the biographer of Freud, first said this.) 'You're not Jewish at all,' he told Taylor in one of their very public fights, 'If there's any Jew in this family, it's me.' 'I AM Jewish', she yelled at him. 'And you can f*** off !' (We've all been there.)

There's a story that soon after her conversion, Liz sought out a publicist on her next film and cheekily said: 'I'm Jewish and I want the day off. If you won't work, I won't either.' Apparently he affectionately replied: 'Elizabeth, you're Jewish until we have our first pogrom.' But she was a devoted friend of Israel her whole life, raising money for the Jewish National Fund and even offering herself as a replacement hostage during the 1976 Entebbe skyjacking.

More recently, Isla Fisher studied for three years to marry Sacha Baron Cohen, taking the Hebrew name Ayala. But it is the example of Margot Stilley, incandescently beautiful star of the frisky film *9 Songs*, whose story is the most intriguing. Drawn to Judaism even before her engagement to a Jew, she said: 'I am not Jewish because I choose to be; I am Jewish because there is no other choice for me.' Interestingly, Miss Stilley rejected Islam, after reading the Koran 'which I found too accepting of violence, constrained by time and place and too vague when it came to feminism.'

Black philo-Semites can often seem few and far between – there is a troubling trend amongst young black men to identify with Islam, which is surely the logic of the madhouse considering Islam's long and shameful role in the enslavement of black nations, right up to Darfur – but when they do get through, they are splendid. Sammy Davis Jr. went so far as to convert – his line 'I'm a black, one-eyed Jew' when asked by a fellow golfer what his handicap was is classic – while in August 2012, talking to the *Financial Times*, Will.i.am revealed that as soon as he could afford to, he moved his family from East Los Angeles to a Jewish neighbourhood in the San Fernando Valley. 'I moved my mom, cousins, my uncles and my grandma. I moved them to the Valley to be near the rabbis. It was either drive-bys or rabbis – I picked the rabbis.' He also has the distinction of being responsible for the only song I know to rhyme *mazel tov* with 'take it off' – an enlivening couplet which I am surprised went begging for so long.

In an amusing, if cringe-worthy footnote, the virulently self-loathing, sorry anti-Zionist actress Miriam Margolyes appeared on a chatshow alongside Mr Am on *The Graham Norton Show* in 2012 when she turned to Will.i.am and said that she was 'fascinated' to meet him – because he was black. Now THAT'S racism. Whereas telling me that it's racist to admire the Jews is as silly and sinister as telling a white fan of say, blues music, that it's racist to admire blues musicians.

If only these same buzz-kills were as fast to pounce on the numerous real manifestations of anti-Semitism which scar society, most of then coming from the hate-merchants of Islamism! Sadly, such alleged anti-racists are much the same as those tragic cultural-relative feminists (thankfully thin on the ground these days) who in the 1980s would be up in arms about being called 'Darlin' by a bus conductor, but who were perfectly accepting of female genital mutilation, as it was part of 'Their' culture. Yeah, and witch-burning, bear-baiting and NO BLACKS signs used to be part of ours – we got over it, and so should 'They.'

There is no entry for philo-Semitism in the *Encyclopaedia Britannica*, nor even in the *Encyclopaedia Judaica*, though both carry extensive pieces on anti-Semitism. Maybe the compilers see us as imaginary creatures, outrageous and unstable as unicorns. Maybe the latter don't want to be seen to be boasting. It wouldn't be the first time Jews have been over-modest about their achievements, or even decried them, for fear of attracting the wrong sort of attention. You can see it in any sad parade, any open letter in the *Guardian* condemning Israel signed by the tragic collectives of Mildly Well-Known Jews For Jihad – Semitic Stockholm Syndrome writ large.

Looking back, I set out determined that I wouldn't let the eternal ugliness of anti-Semitism get into this chapter – that it would just be positive – yet it has. Inevitably, perhaps – as much as philo-Semitism starts as looking at the Jews and thinking 'I'd like to be like that', it also stems from witnessing anti-Semites – from seeing pictures of the death camps to hearing the young Left-wing acquaintance who said to me a few years back, not knowing me well, 'Imagine if the Jews didn't exist – all the trouble that could be prevented!' and thinking shudderingly, 'I never, ever want to be like that.' And knowing that, for so many of your kind, anti-Semitism was the obvious choice. And being so grateful that you'll never understand why.

My son is half Jewish. The half of him that isn't is me. The other half is his father, a Jew, who took him from me in a divorce court when he was nine years old. Though my son is living with me as I write this, he is essentially lost to me forever, divided long ago in an inverted horror parody of the Judgement of Solomon. But I still have my philo-Semitism, and I will hold it to me tight till the day I die. And on that day, you can finally wrap me in that flag for good and lay me down to rest.

TWO

FINDING OUT

They say you never get over your first love and in my case,
They were right. But, typically greedy, my first love was a
whole race of people – the Jews. What started it? I was
a blonde, popular, well-parented West Country schoolgirl,
about as likely a convert to militant Zionism as Daphne
from *Scooby Doo*.

From what I can understand, I feel that I was most
likely zapped, galvanized, struck by some invisible light-
ning of mind-restructuring incredulity at That Moment,
aged fourteen, when I came across the instalment of my
dad's *The World At War* partwork which – dealt with?
exposed? explained? – even at this distance, some forty
years on, I can't find the right word, and I'm quite good
with words – the Holocaust. It described, in simple words
which hid a teeming and complex horror, the systematic
butchering of six million European Jews. But the best
description of the Holocaust I have read can be found
today at Yad Vashem, the Israeli museum of and monu-
ment to what happened:

The Holocaust was the murder by Nazi Germany of six million Jews. While the Nazi persecution of the Jews began in 1933, the mass murder was committed during World War II. It took the Germans and their accomplices four and a half years to murder six million Jews. They were at their most efficient from April to November 1942 – 250 days in which they murdered some two and a half million Jews. They never showed any restraint, they slowed down only when they began to run out of Jews to kill, and they only stopped when the Allies defeated them.

There was no escape. The murderers were not content with destroying the communities; they also traced each hidden Jew and hunted down each fugitive. The crime of being a Jew was so great, that every single one had to be put to death – the men, the women, the children; the committed, the disinterested, the apostates; the healthy and creative, the sickly and the lazy – all were meant to suffer and die, with no reprieve, no hope, no possible amnesty, nor chance for alleviation.

Most of the Jews of Europe were dead by 1945. A civilization that had flourished for almost 2,000 years was no more. The survivors – one from a town, two from a host – dazed, emaciated, bereaved beyond measure, gathered the remnants of their vitality and the remaining sparks of their humanity, and rebuilt. They never meted out justice to their tormentors — for what justice could ever be achieved after such a crime? Rather, they turned to rebuilding: new families forever under the shadow of those absent; new life stories, forever warped by the wounds; new communities, forever haunted by the loss.

The World At War was the greatest documentary series ever shown on British TV, starting in 1973 and concluding in 1974. Episode 20, which was shown in March 1974, was called, simply, 'Genocide'. The magazine I held now in my hands showed me what I had missed on the screen while I was sulking and plotting in my bedroom, as I invariably was most evenings at the age of 14.

Those photographs, in all probability, shut down and then re-booted my brain in some way — I remember feeling dizzy as I looked at them, the room dissolving in a shimmering dark haze around me, and the ground shifting beneath my feet. I don't know how much time passed before I placed the magazine back carefully among the other parts of the partwork. I remember going into the bathroom and staring at my blank, big-eyed face in the mirror (my bedroom looking-glass, in front of which I ceaselessly adored myself, seemed totally inappropriate at that moment) and being surprised that I hadn't changed on the outside, when the rest of me was so different.

In years to come I would learn that this was a novelistic cliché regarding the loss of female virginity — looking in the mirror and expecting to see a different face. I can't speak for anyone else, but I've only experienced this after finding out about the Shoah. All I got from losing my virginity was a sensation of absolute bafflement that anyone would ever want to do this for fun.

Why hadn't I found out about this at school yet? I wondered. I was 14, practically a grown-up. Because no one saw fit to tell me about it, for some reason. And over the next three years, until I left school at 17, no one ever would. I was taught about the Corn Laws and the Spinning Jenny and a lot of other dross which basically gave me a blank cheque to tune out and bunk off – so maybe, just MAYBE, I missed it. But my third husband went to school 13 years later than me, and as a teenager in the 80s, he didn't learn about the Holocaust in History either. Rather, he found out about the Holocaust from his maverick RE teacher Miss Drury, who told her class about it off-schedule.

Whatever: from that moment of part-work revelation – of what happens to Jews if they believe they can trust Whitey – I was already on my way to being on my way, insofar as a land-locked pre-pubescent could ever be. I was packing up my childish effects in the spotted hanky of my tiny, shiny mind and getting set to hit that one-way trail to the Promised Land.

From there on, the evidence just mounted up. The unfairness and cruelty towards them from all corners of the world. The stoicism, intelligence and eventually the hard, cold anger – steeped in stoicism and intelligence – they reacted with. Yes, I was a popular, well-parented little blonde girl from the West Country who grew up loving the Jews, as Patti Smith's poem 'Judith' puts it, 'like the Jews love the land.' When I recalled the Yom Kippur war the year before, I was amazed. What would it take for these people to be left in peace? This tiny country – the size of Wales, I marvelled – build on the blood of six million Jews, butchered like animals while the world stood by, whose only crime had been to believe that it was possible to live unpersecuted in the countries of Europe. And it now seemed to act as a living litmus test for all the envy and evil in the world, bullied by a new bunch of tyrants, filthy rich and democracy-free. But incredibly, as the tyrants' skins were darker than the Israelis, they were in many eyes the Good Guys, the bullied, the wretched of the earth being kicked around from pillar to post by the Zionazis.

This was my first experience of what as a smart-aleck hack I would come to call Paint-Chart Politics. Thus democratic Israel, which gives full civil rights to women and gays, is worse than the countries which surround it, which oppress said women and gays to the point of genocide – but are darker-skinned. Similarly, in Darfur the Left were thrown a curveball when it turned out that the Arab Muslims were terrorising the black Christians. Um, Islam good, Christianity bad – but hang on, Christians darker here! DOES NOT COMPUTE!

Furthermore, I believe that a lot of females who are attracted to the Palestinian and other Islamist causes, often to the point of converting to Islam – which, logically, makes about as much sense as those dozy cows who get their kicks from writing love-letters to assorted serial rapists and murderers of women on Death Row – started off on this rocky road to self-immolation because their heads were turned by televisual interpretations of the sexy sheikh myth at an early age. (And myth it most certainly is:

have you SEEN the state of the men of the ruling families of most of the Middle Eastern fiefdoms? Not being nasty, but they greatly resemble Nazi cartoons of Jews.) But I, ever smart, never thrilled to the Turkish Delight ads as a child, preferred the saucy solitary fellatrix of the Flake ads instead. It's like even then I knew that if a Mohammedan is searching for one's clitoris, it's probably not in order to give a girl some fun, but rather in order to chop it off.

Later on, I remembered the 1972 Munich Olympic massacre from when I was 12 – I hadn't understood then the grotesqueness of Arabs murdering Jews in Germany. They were even given logistical assistance by local Neo-Nazis, to make it even more perfectly vile. When Golda Meir, then Prime Minister of Israel, appealed to other countries to 'save our citizens and condemn the unspeakable criminal acts committed', King Hussein of Jordan was the only leader of an Arab country to denounce the attack, calling it a 'savage crime against civilization...perpetrated by sick minds.' During the subsequent memorial service for the murdered athletes, the Olympic flag was flown at half-mast, along with the flags of most of the other competing nations – except for the ten Arab nations who objected to their flags being lowered to honour Israelis.

I took to brooding in my room for hours about the endless list of indignities and atrocities committed against the Jews, with a level of dedication I had previously only brought to brooding over the supreme unfairness not being old enough to marry Marc Bolan. One day, I decided I'd had enough: I was going to COME OUT and declare my solidarity with Israel. But as my schoolmates probably thought that it was some sort of household detergent, the dolts, or even worse that vile nasty scratchy school toilet paper called Izal, I was reduced to doing it to my mother, in the kitchen, after tea one afternoon, while she was washing up.

'You know the Jews?' I enquired casually, leaning back against the washing machine and savouring the sensation of the spin-dryer going through its paces.

'What street?'

'It's not a FAMILY,' I huffed, cross that she had spoiled my big moment. 'The Jews. The Israelis. They're a RACE.'

'Oh. The Jews. What about 'em?'

I took a deep breath. 'I'm gonna marry one when I grow up.'

My mother turned slowly, tea towel in hand. and if she'd had a lorgnette she'd have peered down it at me. She regarded me with such a level of suspicious disbelief that you'd think I'd just announced that I was planning to marry the Pope, and then ride away with him on a uni-corn to Timbuktu. 'Where biss thee gonna find a ruddy Jew round 'ere?' she challenged rudely. Not for the first time, I reflected on what a cruel joke Mother Nature had played on not just mother but more importantly on me, saddling me with an accent which made the sharpest *bon mot* sound like a straw-sucking yokel's scrumpy-induced idiocy.

Looking back, I see her point. At the time, I was full of righteous teenage rage and went virtually cross-eyed with anger at the fact that mothers hadn't changed since the days of my favourite novel, Mary McCarthy's *The Group*, which chronicles the lives of a set of upper-middle-class American WASP women before the Second World War:

None of them, if she could help it, was going to marry a broker or a banker or a cold-fish lawyer...they would rather be wildly poor and live on salmon wiggle than be forced to marry one of those dull purplish young men of their own set. It would be better, yes, they were not afraid to say it, though Mother gently laughed, to marry a Jew if you loved him – some of them were awfully interesting and cultivated, though terribly ambitious...

Lucky old fictional pre-War posh girls, I reflected bitterly as I ran up the stairs and slammed the door. Hearing it, the dog – innocent barky bystander to many a cross-generational tussle, who by now didn't know whether to whimper or wag when it witnessed one, as the outcome was sometimes that it would be summarily put on its lead and taken out for a walk in a vain bid to assist one side or other in cooling down – yelped in its sleep. It was having a nightmare. So was I. It was called living in a freaking Jew-free zone!

It's a good job the Internet didn't exist then as I would have driven myself even crazier than I was already, Googling 'Jews In Bristol' and then, of course, being far too shy to approach the living ones which would have essentially rendered them as lost to me anyway as the original Bristol Jewish community of 1,100, as recorded in Alex Schlesinger's very helpful paper on the subject. I would have cried over the fate of my city's first rabbi, Moses of Bristol, who with his son Yom-Tov (which now, because of my Hebrew classes, I understand means 'Good Day') was martyred during the York pogram of 1190, and sighed admiringly over another Bristol, Samuel Ha Nackden, who wrote a book about grammar called 'Dekayut.' (Grammar at school = boring rubbish; grammar by Jews = girt lush.)

I would have been very happy indeed to discover that Bristol, unlike Norwich, Gloucester and Bury St Edmunds (of all the unlikely places, it being sitcom shorthand for a place where nothing dramatic could ever happen – but this is what foreigners we are by nature in our own land, blithely unaware of the past, as we glide composedly from dry cleaner to discotheque in the bloody footsteps of murderers and martyrs) did not succumb to the mass hysteria of the 'ritual murder' lie when this charge was made against our Jews in 1183 (to this day, I find it hard to think of a convicted Jewish child-killer – though no doubt some disinterested Truther out there will be more than happy to put me right). But sure as eggs is rotten eggs, the Jews have never been able to trust Whitey for long, and in 1210 the crown patronage they had enjoyed was withdrawn when King John, requiring extra cash for his Irish war, slapped a massive tax on them. When a Bristol merchant named Abraham refused, he was taken to Bristol Castle and one tooth was pulled out for each day of resistance. After seven days, Abraham paid the king the equivalent of seven million pounds. And you thought your dentist was expensive...

Because if I didn't laugh, I'd cry – and frequently do, whenever I attempt to seriously study my favourite subject. What must it be like to be a Jewish child, learning Jewish history? Because stuff like this is on every page. BECAUSE STUFF LIKE THIS IS RELATIVELY MILD. It seems that every other people from the Christians to the Muslims took the blood of the Jews and wrote their history in it. Because you can do that to people, when they have no place they can call their own, no home to go to.

So many big towns and cities have a street called, simply, Jew Street. When I was a teenager, and still raw from finding out, it would make me flinch when I'd see the JEW STREET sign in Bristol, and in other places in England I'd visit to report on the antics of some bunch of singing ninnies for the *NME*. Why can't they call it Jewish Street? I'd think. It's so much more POLITE. But of course the story of the Jews in any country is not a polite one. Some of those buried in the Jewish cemetery outside the Bristol city limits are believed to have been killed during the anti-Jewish riots of 1275, when their quarter was burned and their synagogue ransacked. In 1290 the Jews were expelled by King Edward I, whose wife Eleanor was a stuck-up Jew-hater. The colourful pageant of our past, our glorious monarchs – the persecution of the Jews is the sticky sediment which glues certain pages of our island story together, and gives the whole thing the stench of spite and savagery.

So it was throughout Europe, so it would be in the lands of the Arabs, and so it was right there in the doorstep of my calf country, Bristol, fair city of (in the words of its coat of arms) virtue and industry. Sang our local troubadours The Wurzels:

Virtute et Industrial
Long live all the brewers
Build more pubs and bettin' shops
Don't waste'n on the sewers

Virtute et Industrial
Let's have another drink
Virtute et Industrial
An' never mind the stink.

As I've mentioned already, imagine the sheer livid indignity of being a teenage schoolgirl, a right little madam, sumptuously immersed in the literary and musical canon of the cool, the sharp and the decadent – and growing up in an environment where literally everyone you meet sounds like the sodding Wurzels. (Except your teachers, and who – snigger – wants to sound like THEM?) Even your parents. O Lord – EVEN YOU? Perish the thought!

'Why bisn't thee get a Saturdee job like every other girl thy age?' Mother calls mutinously through the door where I skulk in my bedroom, curtains closed resolutely against the common sun. Who really should get his hat on, as advertised in that stupid Jonathan King song, and make it a big one, because from where I'm sitting he has NOTH-ING to recommend him.

'Because, Mother', I trill back – I call her Mother, partly to get a rise out of her, and partly to make it very clear indeed that there is absolutely no chance of us two being anything horrid such as 'friends' – 'I have another chapter of *The Picture Of Dorian Gray* to finish today. Tomorrow I plan to begin J.K. Huysmans' *A Rebours* – which you may know as *Against Nature*. So obviously I have little leisure time left in which to sweep some suburban sweatshop floor free of fossilized perm cuttings. Comprendez?'

'I'll give 'ee *Against Nature*!' Mother mumbles as she stumbles off, Caliban in drag with a Dust Devil. 'Lazy cow!'

This is the backdrop against which I moon after the Jews, who grow more exotic and crush-worthy by the day in the face of such workaday Wurzeldom. The idea that I too may be made to settle down to a life of Capodimonte-dusting drudgery makes me blush furiously on my own behalf, and wish that I too were part of an exotic, clever, bookish tribe of wanderers. Seeing *Ivanhoe* on TV during this time, I am very taken with the young Elizabeth Taylor, playing the Jewess Rebecca seven years before I was born. How insipid Joan Fontaine's snub blonde Saxon looks are compared to her vivid beauty! Later I will discover that Taylor converted to Judaism seven years after making the film. She explained in her memoirs: 'It had absolutely nothing to do with my past marriage to Mike Todd or my upcoming marriage to Eddie Fisher, both of whom were Jewish. It was something I had wanted to do for a very long time.' But in the meantime I take to winding white pillowcases from the ironing pile around my hair when my parents are out, and practising looking soulfully Semitic in the mirror whereas once I wanted only to look sexy. I realize that Semitically soulful has become what I think of AS sexy.

But where on earth – or rather, in Bristol, will I ever find a real one, one I can have and hold and talk with – with lots of gesticulation, please! – rather than just my own sad shiksa reflection? The gap between Gentiles and Jews in all but a few wealthy parts of England – due to the rapid upward economic movement of the initial wretchedly poor Jewish immigrants – is so vast that the working-class people I grew up with would not knowingly meet a Jewish person in their lifetime, the way they would members of other immigrant groups.

I wouldn't know (but I do now, thanks to Alex Schlesinger's humbling online history of My People x 2) that by the 1540s a covert community of Jews lived in Bristol once more, tolerated so long as they kept their heads down and their services secret, and that one Joachim Ganz, a Bohemian mining engineer got into an argument with a vicar in 1581 during which he dared to let it be known that he was Jewish. Brought before the city elders for this outrageous behaviour, he stated that he was indeed a Jew, and NEVER BAPTIZED! Sent to London for his sins, he 'obligingly repeated the performance before the authorities in the capital.' Shortly afterwards, he was deported.

Some half-wits have sought to forward the feeble-minded notion that Muslims in modern Britain are 'the New Jews', in terms of persecution. I shall deal with this lie – and the clowns who seem intent on spreading it – later in this work, but let us marvel for a moment at the difference in the way Jews were treated then and Muslims are treated now. Even the craziest foreign-born Islamist hate-preacher is showered with all the benefits the Welfare State can lay before him, stopping just short of gold-plated camels and harems of burka-clad dancing girls. Al Qaeda gangs who plotted mass murder in this country have so far been the beneficiaries of British legal aid totalling more than £30 million. Muslim men charged with driving offences have been let off by judges when they explain that they have two wives, and were hurrying between the pair of them. Recent press has been full of stories of Northern English girl children being routinely raped, pimped and tortured by Muslim gangs – maybe mindful of the Koranic teaching that infidel women may be defiled and enslaved with impunity by Islamic conquerors – with the full knowledge of police and social workers, who hold back lest 'community relations' may be damaged. The Archbishop of Canterbury considers Sharia law not beyond the Pale, dear chap, not at all. Yet Jews – 'the Old Muslims', presumably – could be deported JUST FOR BEING JEWS! Once again, the comparison is so crass, so crude, so downright cruelly ignorant, that one is not sure whether tears of fury or hoots of derision are the appropriate response.

When the Jews came back to Britain in 1656, many of them entered through the port of Bristol. (Had I read this part of Alex Schlesinger's history as a horny teenybopper, this is when I would have licked my lips, wriggled in my seat, and swallowed hard – and all the while despising my parents' apparently ceaseless 'divertissement' downstairs at the *Carry On* oeuvre. Kids, eh?) But shockingly, though not surprisingly (the eternal fact of Jewish history), there was no mention of a community for the next century apart from an advertisement for a 'Jews burying ground behind a house in St Philips.'

In 1754 came Bristol's last recorded example of mass anti-Semitism – a protest by the obviously incompetent 'Merchant Venturers' sent to Parliament to stop the proposed naturalization of the Jews. In their indignant incompetence and their special pleading to exclude the dynamic Hebrew outsider, do we not see an echo of the small shops-versus-Tesco scuffle which has kept us moderately entertained over the past decade? In 1919, after serving with the Royal Flying Corps during the First World War, 21-year-old Jack Cohen invested his £30 demob payment in surplus food stocks and a stall in the East End of London. On his first day he had a £4 turnover and made £1 profit; today £1 in every £8 spent by shoppers in this country is handed over to the chain of stores he started. But the idea that Tesco was always a corner-shop-crushing colossus is a lie, one perpetuated by bitter, third-rate businessmen who would dearly love to have achieved a quarter of what Cohen did but lack the ability and luck to pull it off, and who now seek to clothe their envy and hypocrisy in the rhetoric of care for the community. But with a bit less moaning and a bit more ingenuity, what's to stop them doing the same? Instead they would rather spend their time whining, in the manner of one Ken Stevens of the Federation of Small Businesses in East Sussex to the *Brighton Argus* newspaper, 'Where they start selling everything cheaper, that can be very damaging.' Damaging to the pockets of self-interested, incompetent fuss-buckets, YES.

But by the consecration of the Temple Street synagogue – exactly a hundred years on from such mean-spirited protectionism – there had been a remarkable rapprochement between the Jews and the Bristolians, represented at the ceremony by various local Christian leaders: 'It must have been one of the first occasions on which members of the churches attended a synagogue service in an official capacity which did not involve an element of surveillance,' winks Schlesinger. The first ever Jewish house at any British public school was founded at Bristol's

Clifton College in 1878, so now Jews too might have the privilege of looking down on and getting an unfair head's start over their more lowly-born brothers, as Gentile boys had had for many centuries. A Board of Guardians and a Jewish Literary Society followed in 1894, and a Zionist Society in 1899. It is telling that even when things were going apparently well with the host community there was still a desire for Zion – a place of safety, often with changed names like someone embarked on a witness protection scheme, having seen some terrible crime.

By 1906 the Jewish population of Bristol was over 800; but by 1914 it fell to 400. This somewhat sinister blip can probably be explained partly by the understandable suspicion of foreigners during the run-up to the first of the German-inflicted world wars – and not without reason. Some one hundred thousand German Jews volunteered to fight for the Fatherland in 1914 – a high proportion of their population in Germany, of whom twelve thousand died in combat and thirty thousand were decorated with military honours. In Bristol, the aftermath of the First World War saw a decline in the wealth and status of the community, moving from one of the most prominent in the country to one of the most obscure.

Somehow, finding out that there are very few Jews in Bristol isn't as depressing as finding out that there are very few Jews in London or Manchester would be. Indeed, beautiful as Bristol is, the idea of a thriving Jewish community there is hard for me to imagine. Try as I might to overcome ethnic stereotyping, it takes a considerable amount of imagination to reconcile the dynamic, over-achieving Jew with the slow-talking, slow-walking Bristolian attitude to life. I've been asked quite a few times over the years whether my love of the Jews came from being an outsider, or whether loving the Jews caused me to become an outsider – what came first, the chicken soup or the pickled egg – and I honestly don't know. But if even an indigenous Gentile such as I was habitually chomping at the bit at the way Bristolians serenely refused to countenance a life outside the limits of the city (during my life I have met lots of people who were born everywhere on earth and have left that place to come to London, Brighton or beyond – I can count the number of them who were from Bristol on one hand), how must such an under-ambitious and over-contented attitude to life have affected such a notoriously striving and mobile people such as the Jews?

Lots of self-pitying fuss-budget scribblers get all dewy-eyed about the alleged 'Land Of Lost Content' when their half-arsed dreams of glory fail to materialize, but these are generally the sort of misery-buckets who tend to feel like Hamlet on the ramparts when faced with a simple decision over what film to see at the local multiplex. When I think back to my idyllic childhood – loving parents, enough money, a swing in the back yard and hamsters galore – I think of it as the most lividly discontented part of my life, and that includes being trapped in a bungalow in Billericay with Tony Parsons for half a decade. And to escape from it, I dreamed of Israel – establishing early in my life my desire for upheaval over a nice quiet time. Interestingly, Housman wrote most of his Shropshire poems which refer to the land of lost content before he had even visited the place; this is what happened with me and the Jews, I suppose.

So I never met a Jew for the entirety of my childhood and early teenage years, even though there were still, according Alex Schlesinger, some four hundred of the beauties knocking around my manor. It's a good job I didn't, looking back, as I would have made seven sorts of stalkery fool hanging around their places of worship.

I had found out that they existed – that was enough. Now I had to get ready to meet them, and then I had to go and find them. That London seemed as good a place as any.

THREE

HIP YOUNG HEBREW GUNSLINGER

'Be yourself.' 'Write about what you know.' From the cradle to the grave, the homespun homilies of honesty are thrust upon one like a jar of potpourri masquerading as a fragrant bouquet, all dusty and redundant yet hopeful of being passed off as an original and inspiring gift that one should go into a regular swoon upon receiving.

But what if you didn't know who you were, apart from a self-defiling teen dream ('You're gonna GET IT tonight!' I would often growl at my gorgeous naked self of a morning as I pulled on my vile school uniform, following with a wide-eyed pout and a finger pointing at my shimmering sternum 'Who, me?' I'd pipe tremulously. Yes, I was WEIRD!) suffering from a chronic case of inappropriate ethnic identification with a people of whom I'd never even come within sniffing distance? And how could you write about what you knew, if you didn't know anything except that you had to get out of the place you were condemned to live in? (No disrespect to my sainted parents.) I read a line in an essay by the great David Sedaris recently, about his sister Gretchen, and it really spoke to me, complete with jazz hands:

It was like having a foreign-exchange student living in our house. Nothing we said or did made any sense to her, as she seemed to follow the rules and customs of some exotic, faraway nation...

The Jews had become a symbol to me of escape – of out-siderness not just embraced, but made magnificent. Now when I went to the library, I wasn't looking up sex things in encyclopaedias, I was looking up stuff about Israel. Right from the beginning, I shied away from the Shoah. I didn't want to know about them being hurt – I wanted to under-stand how they came to be strong. My blind uncritical love of Israel, which accepted (and indeed accepts to this day) without question every last thing it does, could be seen (by an unfriendly type who more than likely has the hots for the opposite team, so THEY can talk) as the way a maths obsessive delights in the ultimate extreme algebra puzzle. It wasn't a crush, like you'd have on a pop star pin-up. It was something you could look at forever, trying to work out, but knowing that you wouldn't actually be missing out on any aspect of if you never made any headway whatso-ever on getting to the root of it, because just looking is so wonderful. To this day I'm the only person I know whose reaction to any result in any Israeli election is 'We won!' whether the first prize was scooped by Left, Right and/or Centre. Just the thought of Jews voting for other Jews strikes me as the most immensely wonderful thing. It's like Portnoy says when he first visits the country, after a lifetime of being around weak and worrying diaspora types; 'Look at the Jewish children laughing, acting as if they own the place...WHICH THEY DO!'

I never sought in the Jews what many other penny-ante philo-Semites seek – 'Jewish warmth' and all that jazz, like poor dumb Mary-Jane in *Portnoy's Complaint*. (The only Jewish warmth I was ever interested in came out of a circumcised cock, frankly.) I don't like Jewish humour, the films of Woody Allen or bagels. I don't think families are the most important thing in the world. I'm not seeking anything FROM the Jews at all, if the truth be told. I am seeking an absence, a mystery, an unknowable something which happened centuries ago which resulted in a tribe of desert nomads surviving for four millennia – while every sucker, charlatan and Sadducee attempted to eradicate them – to basically build the modern world. A tribe which then imagined itself into triumphant re-birth as a nation, combative and contrary as all get-out, after ceaseless centuries of roaming in the wilderness. (And there is more than one sort of wilderness.) Just how DID a desert tribe, apparently not that much different from any other bunch of Biblical primitives, come out of a bleak, bullied walkabout as what looks to me very much like the next step in the evolution of Mankind? Put simply, the Jews were never forgiven for making the rest of mankind look like monkeys in comparison. And ooo, ooo, ooo, I so DID want to be like them...

Looking back over what I've written here, there is of course an elephant in the room – especially in my bedroom. Apart from that playful pachyderm named masturbation which – hot as hell and determined to keep myself tidy for what lay ahead (I stole that line from Princess Diana!) – I become a veritable virtuoso at from the age of 12, sometimes giving myself such a good seeing too that I land on the floor beside my bed with a profoundly childish BUMP and scurry sneakily back under the covers again as my mum calls up the stairs 'OI! You got a baby elephant up there?'

But even more than masturbation, I mean music. Music was the noisiest elephant in the room as I hit adolescence, and the one thing I loved as much as the Jews and abusing myself. Sometimes, gazing at my posters of Marc Bolan (a Jew! Neé Feld, son of Simeon!), I found it hard to know where music ended and masturbation began. And that was the magic of being a teenager in a naughty old nutshell. When you're a kid, a teenager, music is like a dream of sex. It's like (as my husband Dan says) standing on a REALLY HIGH ROOFTOP for the first time and looking out and seeing all manner of fantastic things you never ever dreamed existed. And – if the music is good enough, if it touches you hard enough in all the soft places – it makes you feel that you can fly.

I started adoring Marc Bolan at the age of 12. Later, when I was a sassy 17-year-old, he would catch my eye in a punk club and smile, and I would look away quickly, as if he could have told just by looking at me all the times as a child I came so hard thinking about him. Spurned by his erstwhile love-slave, and to be honest by the self-consciously cool crowd in general (who probably ALL masturbated over his image as kids) he mooched around the club alone for a little longer and then left alone – just like in 'How Soon Is Now'! – and soon he died a rock star's death, wrapped around a tree in a speeding car. Ah, the fickleness of self-fiddling youth!

But in the early 70s – from 'Ride A White Swan' in 1971 to 'Twentieth Century Boy' in 1973 – there is nothing I wouldn't have done for this doe-eyed, sucky-cheeked, glitter-dusted man-boy. I mean ANYTHING. The things I thought up for us to do, should we ever have had the good fortune to be locked in a lavatory together, from Monday to Saturday just like in the nursery rhyme, make my blood run cold even now to countenance. And I've been married three times. Though it's a wonder it wasn't four times, as I distinctly recall – after reading one Dennis Wheatley too many – drawing a risibly inept pentagram on a bit of school graph paper one night when my parents were innocently imbibing at the local hostelry The Good Intent, and solemnly promising my soul to Beelzebub if he fixed it for me to marry Marc B when I came of age. Just think, if I'd have smiled back that night at the Vortex, I could be one of your actual Damned by now! And I don't mean the rubbish punk group, either.

Anyway, during these couple of years I would buy anything with his face on. That included a horrible boring-looking newspaper-type-thing called the *New Musical Express*, with no colour photos you could properly touch yourself up over, and dirty black ink that came off on one's pinkies anyway. (The idea of getting ink on one's clitoris was appalling to me at the age of twelve. Later, it would seem...not so bad AT ALL.) I was beyond delighted to find a three-part interview with him by someone called Nick Logan, which contained SWEARING! Swearing, AND one's masturbatory idol – does life get any better, I wondered, as I abused myself to it for the nth time?

A word about the *NME* here. It was selling more than 300,000 copies a week back then and had the unmistakeable rough-beast swagger of a magazine whose time has come. Now it sells less than 24,000 and looks like some free-sheet you'd see left, undefiled, on the bus. But in 1972, somehow, for reasons it itself did not seem to understand – it had been around since 1952, and had quite recently been wetting its collective knix at the sight of Helen Shapiro sharing a joke with Joe Loss – it had become a sort of World Service of Hip, and would remain so until the 80s, when the new glossies prised the baton of the zeitgeist from its pale, clammy hand. Decades later I met a boy from New Zealand (pleasingly named David Cohen) and he expressed the way most *NME* readers who lived beyond the exciting 'burgs of London and New York felt; 'Can you imagine being 15 and just sitting on this rock at the end of the world? And then every week this paper arrives, and you actually feel PART of the world for once?'

Happily, David C got back in touch with me through the wonder of Facebook while I was writing this, and I asked him to elaborate further. He said the following – the last bit of which is a testimony to my extreme Zionism even in my SWP late teens, *The Boy Looked At Johnny* having been published in 1978.

Regarding the NME: *it's hard to overstate what a cultural staple this was for younger New Zealanders in the 1970s and '80s. It was very expensive in those days, so any British publication typically took up to four months to arrive in the antipodes. And, of course, given how quickly new trends were being discovered and then ditched by the paper's writers, it often happened that the smart set who read it here would be latching on to acts who had long been consigned to the rubbish bin back in the UK. So you had this kind of looooong echo thing going on in the antipodes, in for example the cases of Joy Division, the Specials, the Smiths and all the rest. But that didn't stop (almost) everyone here lapping it up, and of course (in the case of rock crits) completely aping the style and content of you guys. I was a terrible offender in this respect, so much so that I can't bear to look at anything I wrote back then about music in my late teens and early 20s because it was so horribly derivative of the same. Nonetheless the culture here would have been much different here without it.*

I remember really enjoying your writing, in particular, because the voice was so distinctive – no derivation there! – and for the fact it was that of a woman working in such an overwhelmingly testosterone-soaked organ. But to be TOTALLY HONEST, what got me the most was line four of the dedications in The Boy Looked At Johnny, *which as a somewhat alienated 17 year old I thought was just stunning, all the more so for the publishers disassociating themselves from it. That took courage, and I think — I hope — in some way it inspired me much more than any of those dear, dead reviews from* NME *in my later work.*

Line four of the dedication in *The Boy Looked At Johnny* was to no less than Menachem Begin; the great Israeli Prime Minister whose Irgun liberation movement was the most militant in its actions against British rule in 'Palestine' — a name for Judea, I was to discover, imposed by the Roman conquerors. The co-author Tony Parsons and I found it amazing and amusing in equal parts as to how the Jewish-owned Left-wing Pluto Press could actually go so far as disassociating themselves from a dedication, which was sure by its nature so personal that such an action was superfluous, to say the least? (Only being young brats of the working-class blood royal, this probably wasn't the way we expressed our contemptuous incredulity to each other at the time — 'Prats!' was probably nearer our considered opinion. But certainly no further from the truth.)

Interestingly, the other quarter from which the most objection came to our dear little dedication was from a fellow working-class music hack, Garry Bushell of *Sounds*. (Even writing that last bit of sentence makes me wince, and I'm not exactly sensitive. It's just so HORRID! You know, you grow up reading Dottie Parker and Ossie Wilde — and you never DREAM that one day you're going to be using exactly the same exquisite tongue in which to grimly etch the words 'Garry Bushell of *Sounds*.') Old Bacon-Bonce got his grotty Y-fronts (one imagines — with a shudder) into a right old twist over it, banging on about Zionist war criminals and what have you. Bushell is most remembered these days for cultivating the Oi! Bands – a gaggle of outfits which arrived as the afterbirth of punk, so very unsophisticated that they made Sham 69 look like the Dave Brubeck Quartet – which eventually brought forth luscious fruit in the blessed year of 1981 in the form of the *Strength Thru Oi!* compilation album, under the auspices of Bacon-Bonce himself. What fun to make a pun on a famous Nazi slogan, and to feature as its cover starlet a British Movement skinhead currently serving a prison sentence for racist violence!

Not the last time I experienced the extraordinary way that extreme right and extreme left would unite against things Jewish, but probably the first...

*

Anyway, back to the past – and the past glories of the *NME* in particular. Long after Marc Bolan had fallen out of favour with my childish fist, I continued to cleave to my *NME* as fiercely as a suicidal baby to a poisoned rattle. All around me the glowing normality of my friends and family showed me how happy and straightforward life could be, if one only expected small pleasures – and I wanted none of it. If I'd had to put it into words, I would have said (in my yokelish lilt) that I wanted to be a poetry-writing junkie dying of consumption in an attic, thank you very much, and could I please be a lesbian too, while you're at it, Santa?

The *NME*'s writers – well, Charles Shaar Murray and Nick Kent, anyway – made my schoolgirlish head swim with the lush, louche lives they appeared to lead. (Years later I discovered CSM to be a hen-pecked husband straight out of a sit-com and Nick Kent to be so half-witted that on regularly bumping into a hat-stand on entering the *NME* office, he apologized to it, but anyway.) AND THEY DIDN'T EVEN HAVE TO PLAY A SODDING MUSICAL INSTRUMENT IN ORDER TO GET THESE LIVES! I knew from various besotted English teachers that I had a way with words – might I somehow use these words to get away?

I was also querying another matter at this time: could one actually MAKE oneself a lesbian by having the hots for oneself too frequently? I was once a regular little girl, kissing boys behind school library shelves (never anything as sordid as bike sheds for ever-bookish little me) and masturbating over caterwauling love totems. But I seemed increasingly interested in girls as I edged through my teens. I had an inkling that it might have been sheer self-preservation; as I became of an age where I might conceivably conceive – and thus up the ante of getting stuck in Nowheresville-on-Severn forever – I shied away from the source of such semen-spread shackledom. Or is it simply that I had fancied myself so often in my full-length Junior Princess dressing-table mirror of a morning that I had gone and turned myself irretrievably queer? All that masturbation – and it had been A GIRL'S HAND DOING IT!

When my mother made coy comments about Boys, I wanted to strike her. Maybe this lesbo-hood was my punishment for upsetting her whenever she attempted to give me a goodnight kiss: 'Father, has it ever occurred to you that Mother may have lesbian tendencies?' I would pipe pompously, pushing her away. When I thought of the ark animals going in two by two, it made me want to retch. What if they had absolutely NOTHING IN COMMON? The unutterable vulgarity of the whole set-up made me wince.

Anyway, like a million other pale teenage self-abusers I saw THAT photo of Patti Smith from the cover of the *Horses* album and can barely sit down for a week. I buy it, don't get it – but I love it anyway. Smith would turn out to be your archetypal beautiful-but-dumb showbiz-kid – saying things like 'There's a real lot of inspiration going on between the murderer and his victim', and slagging off Israel like a thing possessed – but for now, my bed was on fire five times a night. And not just because of the drought. Sticky with ambition and lust, I tossed and turned in my virginal bed all night long. But especially tossed.

In the long hot summer of July 1976, they prayed for rain in the churches of the West Country. So did I – a flood, something, ANYTHING to sweep me clean away from this lovely place and my wonderful parents into the fetid embrace of unkind strangers.

In Uganda, at Entebbe Airport, Palestinian and German hijackers – of all the countries in the world, of all the terrorists in the world, Palestinians HAD to hook up with Germans to kill Jews! – separated Jewish and non-Jewish passengers on the Air France aeroplane they have hijacked, as they chose who will die first. Was it back? Or did it never really end?

I completed my O Levels and agreed to go back and do my A Levels in September – anything would be better than getting a job in the sodding BISCUIT FACTORY and ADMITTING DEFEAT. I read That Piece by the Man Who Passed For Jewish in *Rolling Stone* magazine, pale with envy. I also turned 17 – WTF! I lay on the grass in the back garden, sulking about how my life was over before it'd began, until a bunch of bastard ants who were obviously in league with my mother made me jump up from my unwholesome idling – and headed straight into the house to have another quick abuse of myself over the sleeve of *Horses*, as luck would have it, after checking that the parents were otherwise employed.

Now that I was 17, masturbation felt sad, whereas it had been the most fun I'd ever had. Once it had made me feel free, but now it felt like a dirty jailer. 'If I met you, I could get away from here', I told the impassive woman whose image I had propped up on my pillow. 'I know I could get away if I met you, and never come back.'

Then a miracle happened, in black and white. For two weeks in July, ignobly jostled by the ads for No Time-wasters and Tie-Dye Shirtwaisters, an ad runs in the *NME*.

Attention hip young gunslingers. The NME *has a vacancy for a STAFF WRITER. Previous experience in either journalism or the music business is not essential, but a good knowledge of rock and enthusiasm are, together with the ability to write lively and incisive prose. All applications must be accompanied by a sample 5–600 word review of any album of the applicant's choice.*

I can do that, I thought. I had a typewriter – 'How's your typing coming on?' my mum was wont to ask, poking her head around the door of the back room where I furiously pounded out fantasies of sex and revenge; 'I'm WRITING, Mum, not TYPING!' I hissed for the nth time – but I decided that I was going to milk my youth for all it was worth. I hand-wrote my *Horses* review on paper torn jaggedly from a schoolbook, and shook my fountain pen over the finished effort for that extra inky-fingered teenage scamp effect. I was stage-managing myself even then, even when the nearest I'd been to a stage was my star turn as the Sailor Doll in a Mixed Juniors panto way back before I grew tits and ambition.

There were more than 15,000 applicants for that job, which of course I didn't know at the time, but even if I'd known there'd been a million, I still would have been sure of getting it. I laughed at my mum's mates who could feel things in their water, but from the moment I posted that envelope addressed to the *New Musical Express*, King's Reach Tower, Stamford Street, London SE1 into the post-box at the top of my street, it was my street no longer. I became like an astronaut in one of those sleeping chambers, frozen, waiting for life to begin. To all intents and purposes I seemed the same; I cheeked my mum, I swore at the dog, I abused myself. But really I was in a trance-state, treading water and biding my time, solemnly contemplating the helter-skelter I had been wanting to throw myself down head-first ever since I heard the word 'London.' Three weeks into my A Levels, in September, I got the job.

I remember Pretendy Jewish Man. Could I become my own Frankenstein – and his creation, too? Yes, I could! I dyed my hair black. I shivered with pleasure at my own reflection, and abused myself extra that night.

Nothing could stop me. I was about to abandon speech – that chunky, clunky second language I had come to loathe – and embrace my mother tongue: writing. And, better yet, I would do it as a Jew. For me at least, the drought was over.

*

For someone as obsessed with honesty as I have become, it never fails to shock me that I went into my job at the *NME* living not just one lie, but two. For starters, I said I loved punk music. Ha! I was a punk of convenience from the start, realizing instinctively that they were looking for some hot young blood to wet-nurse them, as it were, through the upcoming and somewhat problematic (to a bunch of wet, middle class hippies, that is) punk movement. The only music that existed for me was black music, and punk was just about the whitest, most sexless and joyless sound I'd ever heard, but I threw away my dancing shoes and grabbed the safety pins PDQ – and thus began my short career as a hypocrite.

But when you're a super-bright working-class girl who knows that following one's mater into the cardboard box factory is DEFINITELY not quite what one is dreaming of, you don't have the luxury of taking decisions at leisure. Unlike the dreary, late-blooming offspring of the middling class, you don't faff away your Fruit Salad chew days pissing around with 'uni' and gap years and sabbaticals until your mid-twenties. You see a ladder coming down from the 'copter, and you CLIMB.

I remember many a night coming home to my scuzzy bedsit in – my dear, how divinely amusing! – 'Crouch

End', my ears ringing with the latest vile white-thrash cacophony, peeling off my dumb-ass punk gear and dancing round the room in my scanties to the cleansing balm of the Isley Brothers 'Forever Gold' on my little red Dansette – free at last of that rotten white racket, free at last! Fortunately, punk would be over within two years – the only good thing about it, in my opinion.

Even more deviously, I had presented myself as a Jew, getting around my yokel piping and resolutely rural place-name surname by claiming my mother as a Polish Jewess called Elizabieta Grynszpan. (I'm actually cringing as I write this, a first for me.) During my library forays into Jewish history, I had been very taken with a photograph of 17-year-old Herschel Grynszpan. He was a beautiful young refugee from Poland who in the striking black and white photographs of him at the time of his notoriety could have been mistaken for a Neurotic Boy Outsider of the crooning or modelling mode, but was in fact famous for the rather more substantial achievement of assassinating the German diplomat Ernst vom Rath on 9 November 1938 in Paris, providing the Nazis with the pretext for Kristallnacht, the pogrom of the 10th and 11th of November which saw Jewish homes, synagogues, shops and businesses destroyed across Germany. In 1944 Sir Michael Tippett's oratorio about him, *A Child of Our Time*, would first be performed. And thirty-two years later, I would tell any of my *NME* colleagues who asked that he was my mother's cousin.

They say imitation is the sincerest form of flattery, and that was certainly true in my case. It makes me laugh to look back at it now. True, I had dyed black hair and a big nose, but with my Somerset twang I was a very strange Jew indeed – all I lacked was the bit of straw sticking out of my mouth and the perfume of muck-spreading on my mitts.

So far as I could make out, there were two real Jews at the *NME*, and though neither of them had Jewish names – Murray and Farren – I knew by now that, incredibly, many Jews were uncomfortable with the bounteous blessing of their ethnicity. Still, I was amazed that they didn't rumble me – they apparently were so alienated from their own roots, I tut-tutted to myself, that they had no Jewdar whatsoever; I remember thinking, shocked, 'Boy, Jews can be dumb too!' It's weird when you meet your first dumb Jew – like meeting a gay man who can't dance – and I've never gotten used to it, right to this day.

FOUR

RUM, *NME*, THE LASH AND ANTI-FASCISM

It's weird how one minute you're a virgin schoolgirl staring at an icon and the next minute you've slipped feet-first into the undertow of your own legend, albeit a minor one, and albeit in your own mind. I certainly had a lot to think about in my new role as teenage punk reporter.

Sex, with Tony Parsons – very disappointing, like having one's foot repeatedly trodden on, I couldn't help thinking. Amphetamine sulphate – every glorious thing sex was MEANT to be, so far as I could see. All those stupid punks running around wearing swastikas, especially that titless wonder Siouxsie of the stupid Banshees – loathsome in the extreme. In 1978, I would write a review of her first album *The Scream* for the *NME*, which contained the following:

Until recently Siouxsie And The Banshees included in their set a song they had written called 'Love In A Void'. This song featured the line 'Too many Jews for my liking'. This, says Siouxsie, was a metaphor for too many fat businessmen waiting to pounce, suck the youth from and cast aside new talent.

I do not see the connection. I, self-righteous square that I am, consider 'Too many Jews for my liking' to be the most disgusting and unforgivable lyric-line ever written, though God knows there has been more appalling filth written within rockanroll than in every other branch of entertainment taken together.

None of it comes anywhere in sight of Siouxsie, though. She is well into her twenties, so ignorant youth is no excuse, however lame. Therefore she must be either evil or retarded – well, can YOU think of any other way out? To shock? No – the pain and dreadful implications of this sentence could only be justified into a means of outrage by aforementioned retard.

Though I know that for a critic to tell the Banshees where to go is as de trop as liking, say, The Runways, I am still particularly disgusted by the way Jewish writers (Viv Goldman) and otherwise extremely moral writers (Chris Brazier) have drooled over the silly cow, letting her get away with that line as long as she promises 'Oh, it was an unwise choice, I'll change it as soon as I can think of something better!'

Well, take your shocking song and stick it up your rude white ass, Sioux, because here's a review that don't believe in running with the pack.

What a junior priss, you might think. But also, what a dear, sweet, principled young woman. I came from a background steeped in straightforward labour and trades union politics, via my dad; I saw a swastika and I didn't see something that could be playful, or 'ironic.' I saw a symbol of evil, and I'm glad I did. I once read a book in which a Native American detective, created by Loren D. Estelman, when accused of seeing things in black and white says something like 'Things have always been black and white. The only people who ever think things are shades of grey are people who've had some of the black rub off on them.' I forgot the name of the book, but I always remember that line.

This was the time when a teenage Tracey Thorn would write her song 'Julie' – 'My ode to Julie Burchill,' she wrote in her autobiography *Bedsit Disco Queen*, 'who I worshipped and adored. I had pinned to my bedroom wall that iconic black-and-white *NME* shot of her and Tony Parsons leaning against a brick wall, though I had ruthlessly cut Tony out of the photo, knowing exactly who the talent was, and my song was written in her defence – as if she needed my help. "Everybody hates you, Julie/Everybody hates you but they can't see/What you're really like, Julie/Everybody hates you – except for me."' Talk about a back-handed compliment!

In Jonathan Coe's book *The Rotters' Club*, published in 2001, I never actually appear but the young hero, going for an interview at the *NME*, espies 'a surreal detail':

The office space had been divided up into cubicles, and on top of one of the partitions someone had laid out a tangle of barbed wire and broken glass. Inside the cubicle itself, between the two desks, a noose was hanging from the ceiling and swaying very slightly from side to side in the moving currents of air.

Richard followed his gaze and said, 'Yeah, that's Tony and Julie's bunker...they just put up that stuff to scare us. They're like naughty kids.'

The kinderbunker was the scene of many a pout, plot and tantrum during the two years Tony and I festered there, enjoying the sumptuous luxury of feeling totally misunderstood on a monthly salary. In recent years our 'feud' has been made much of, but I always saw us as far more akin to Bette Davis and Joan Crawford than some star-crossed Sicilian bandit types. There is often something very camp about men concerned with being overtly masculine, and though I couldn't properly have put this into words, it was what made me like Tony's company – AS A FRIEND! – so much.

He was possibly the only person more self-dramatizing than myself than I had ever met – including my mother! – except I had the alibi of being a 17-year-old girl, whereas he was in his mid-20s and had travelled through Europe, had a pulp novel published and worked in a gin distillery. What was HIS excuse for acting like Violet Elizabeth Bott with PMT? OK, so not long ago I personally had run amok, crying and screaming and kicking over any waste-paper bins I could find when a posse of unfortunate dwarves had been sent up to the *NME* office to publicize some hopeless new act, in order to protest at the 'exploitation' involved. It had taken all six dwarves to calm me down and cheer me up, bless their tiny cotton socks! But I WAS 17. I was literally disenfranchised – no wonder I was easily upset.

TP was quite capable of moping round the kinderbunker for days on end – probably because I had made it clear that under no circumstances, including threat of death or us being the last male and female left in the universe, did I wish to repeat the unfortunate sexual experience which had removed my pesky virginity – before sitting down at his desk to scribble something on a bit of paper, with many a sigh, a squirm and a furtive glance at me. It was either unrequited love or piles, and he was wondering how to ask me to go to the chemist for him.

Instead he leapt up and thrust the page into my hand. I squinted at it suspiciously – and immediately recognized a snippet of lyrics from the song 'Easy To Be Hard', a song sung by a pregnant hippie girl character in the musical *Hair*. Back in Bristol, my mum's friend Jo-Next-Door, who was Mildly Racy, had the album and had lent it to me when I was 13.

How can people have no feelings?
How can they ignore their friends?
Easy to be proud, easy to say no
And especially people who care about strangers
Who care about evil and social injustice
Do you only care about the bleeding crowd?
How about a needing friend?
I need a friend.

My lips set in a grim parody of my mother's on surveying the latest of my antics. He HAD a friend – me. What he didn't have was access to his friend's genitalia any hour of the day and night – or even once in a blue moon on the twelfth of never, come to that – which was obviously playing havoc with his hormone levels. A few weeks ago, he had seen Iggy Pop – previously his best buddy, to hear HIM talk, after a riotous weekend in Amsterdam courtesy of *NME* expenses in hot pursuit of a cover story – touch my leg, and had subsequently given the Iggster a handful of laxatives which he pretended were speed pills JUST BEFORE Little Jimmy Jewel was due to headline at the Hammersmith Odeon. Mr Pop had utilized several stage props in the course of his long career – peanut butter, broken glass – but I doubt if a bucket of muck in the wings had ever featured strongly in his act before.

My lip curled as I re-read the 'social injustice' jibe – THIS was obviously a none too subtle poke at my recent concern over the ascendance of the National Front, and my intention to attend the counter-demonstration in Lewisham soon. Tony had announced his intention of coming with me, ostensibly as a fellow anti-fascist, but no doubt to ensure that I didn't cop off with a big black man while fighting the good fight. When would he get it through his head that one swallow didn't make a relationship?

I handed it back; 'It's that song from *Hair*. That the pregnant hippie girl sings.'

He shot me a shocked look, appalled at being caught out impersonating a pregnant hippie girl. 'Is it? I wouldn't know. *HAIR!*' he guffawed weakly.

I wasn't listening. Mick Farren, one of the Two Jews – the other was Charles Shaar Murray – who had the office cubicle next to ours, had reeled in late, as usual. I could hear his gravelly, asthmatic voice as he joshed jovially with the seccies at Reception, and I came over all unnecessary.

In theory, we hated the Two Jews for being old and hippies. (CSM was in his twenties, Farren in his thirties!) In practice, I was living in the spare bedroom of the first and desperately plotting to move into the bedroom of the second, albeit for just one night. This didn't stop me from frequently scrambling up onto Tony's desk, which was pushed up against our mutual partition with them, and competing with TP to flick lighted cigarillo butts off the top of it into their Afros – or 'Isros' rather – whenever we were bored. How strange and tormented my attempts to express my adoration to the Chosen had already become!

Not half as tormented as it would, I gloated, as Mickey wheezed past, creakily resplendent in his leather trousers. While Tony was busy copying out the entire lyrics from *Hair* in order to win my love, I was casting lustful glances at the beautiful wreck now swaggering past my cubicle with a casual 'Awlright, sweetheart?'

I snickered winsomely and started singing my current favourite song quietly to myself, Blue Oyster Cult's 'Career Of Evil'. (I had more or less given up pretending to like punk by the summer of '77 – I said it was to do with the Clash signing to CBS or some other utter bollocks.) In my Caramac Bunny accent and child's voice, the lyrics must have sounded well freaky:

I plot your rubric scarab, I steal your satellite

I want your wife to be my baby tonight
I choose to steal what you chose to show
And you know I will not apologize
You're mine for the taking
I'm making a career of evil
CAREER OF EVIL!

I had already repaid CSM's hospitality by getting off with his wife, so I sniggered knowingly at this as I edged out of the kinderbunker and left Tony to his Broadway show-tunes lyric-copying. Maybe he'd move on to *West Side Story* next, and present me with the precious love token of the lyrics to 'Maria', only changed to 'Ju-LI-a.' Clown!

I sidled up to the doorway and got an eyeful of Mickey. CSM once wrote of him that 'Farren could never quite make up his mind whether he wanted to be Lord Byron, Gene Vincent, Leon Trotsky, Bob Dylan, Dylan Thomas, William S Burroughs, or Harlan Ellison; though he would probably have settled for being the pre-bloat-and-flame-out incarnation of Jim Morrison. In the end, he had to settle for being Mick Farren.' To my mind, that was a far preferable fate to being like a bunch of club-footed, lame, junkie poets with ice-picks through their heads, glamorous though such options obviously were.

Pay me – I'll be your surgeon, I'd like to pick your brains
Capture you, inject you, leave you kneeling in the rain
I choose to steal what you chose to show

And you know I will not apologize
You're mine for the taking
I'm making a career of evil
CAREER OF EVIL!

I sang in my head as I wriggled and posed, posed and wriggled in what I imagined to be a wanton way in the Two Jews' doorway. In my mind's eye I Biblically captioned it YULIA THE WHORE OF BRISTOL, BEING OFFERED UP TO THE SONS OF ZION. But I probably looked more as if I had Saint Vitus Dance. CSM spotted me first and did this little-cat's-asshole thing with his mouth. He SO knew what was on my dirty mind; I fancied his friend. And despite the fact that I was 17 and his friend was pushing 40, he knew who the bruiser was, and instinctively flinched from it.

On paper, Charlie and Mickey were quite similar – on all fours, they couldn't have been more different. Charlie was plump, pink and petulant – but Mickey was a staggering welterweight without a cause, who seemed both dangerous and attractive because he seemed genuinely to despair of life while never, ever whining about it. And in my book, especially this one, self-pity in a man is to sex what a bucket of cold water is to a pair of copulating dogs.

I bet he wouldn't copy the lyrics from a fictional pregnant hippie girl's lament and try to pass it off as some sort of cri de sodding coeur, I sneered inwardly. Indeed, I knew for a fact that he and a gang of fellow degenerates and subversives once lived in a flat above the Shaftesbury Theatre while *Hair* was playing. He was the real McCoy, and I intended to get a piece of him. Rumour was that he was a sadist. A Jewish sadist! I felt my eyes start to cross with lust and made a determined effort to set them right.

'Mickey...I'm bored.' I indicated the large BORED TEENAGER badge which I had chosen to wear not on my chest – too obvious, and besides my nipples had enough to say on their own behalf without encouraging sloganizing – but rather pinned to my upper thigh, about three inches from my be-denimmed genitalia. Subtlety, thy name is teenage lust! 'Have you got...anything for me?'

Murray rolled his eyes.

Mickey got out the Sinex spray which he used about once every ten minutes. IN FLAGRANT CONTRADIC-TION OF THE INSTRUCTIONS ON THE BOX! I gaped at him, lost in sheer molten lust at his swashbuckling abuse of over-the-counter medicines. Whenever he looked at me, he seemed to wince slightly. I took this as attraction; I was, literally, a sight for sore eyes, my youth livid and really quite heartbreaking in some ways, my mind and body unstretched. He had said a thing to me, in a taxi, when we were drunk, that struck me as the most brilliant, sexually exciting thing I had ever heard – a world away from the 'Nice tits!' and 'Come over 'ere and SIT ON IT!' which I had become used to on the monosyllabic streets of Bristol.

'You will die alone – like Virginia Woolf.'

He was already comparing me to characters played by Elizabeth Taylor, in famous films, and I was still only 17! I had indeed come a long way, baby, from my pristine provincial band-box. And if I was really lucky, I might catch VD by Christmas! I fell into a reverie just thinking about what the clinic might smell like. And I might get a

JEWISH DOCTOR, who would be FILLED WITH CON-
TEMPT for me, yet find me STRANGELY IRRESISTIBLE
as he...

'Cab it up to Old Compton Street, sweetheart, and get
us a bunch of magazines. Everything from *Guns & Ammo*
to *Paris Match*. Then come back and fillet 'em and see if
you can write up a few items for Teazers.'

Teazers was the *NME* gossip column/diary/unusual
snippets pages; I was now pretty much confined to bar-
racks working for it, under the auspices of my darling
Mickey, having slipped a cheeky soupcon of amphetamine
sulphate into Country Joe McDonald's tea when I was
rudely sent to interview him. I had had nothing I wanted
to ask him, and was curious as to how I would manage to
go back to the office with a sentence, let alone a scoop. My
modus operandi in the few interviews I had done for the
NME so far was to turn on my tape recorder and then stare
silently at the subject until they said something. The first
time, with Boney M, it has worked brilliantly, as there was
also a girl along from *Record Mirror* called Robin Katz –
a great Jewish name! – who took pity on my mute horror, did a sensationally assured interview with them and
slipped me her tape of it on the way out 'as it's your first
time.'

What a menschette! But sadly, subsequent interviews
did not end so fortuitously – Robin Katz not being con-
stantly available to act as my representative on earth – so
by the time I was sent to get something resembling a story
from my encounter with this old hippie, I was desperate
for inspiration. On the Tube on the way to see Country Joe,
mind racing from that cheeky morning line, I realized that

amphetamine sulphate got even a shy little violet like me talking a mile a minute, and wondered if it might not have the same effect on an interviewee. Well, we'd soon see!

Sadly my experiments in basic chemistry were brought to an abrupt ending when a spoil-sport minder of CJ's saw my little sleight of hand and reported me to the editor, earning me a stern carpeting and a ban on doing interviews. Which was, of course, just fine by me. No longer did I have to waste my time on prising out words far closer to plastic poppet-beads than pearls from the lips of various musical sad-sacks, seat-sniffers and bed-wetters, but instead was free to read foreign magazines every day and perve over Mickey, AND get paid for it. Truly I was in teenage heaven.

I'd like your blue-eyed horseshoe, I'd like your emerald horny toad
I'd like to do it to your daughter on a dirt road
And then I'd spend your ransom money, but still I'd keep your sheep
I'd peel the mask you're wearing, and then rob you of your sleep
I choose to steal what you chose to show
And you know I will not apologize
You're mine for the taking
I'm making a career of evil
CAREER OF EVIL!

I read an interesting thing once by Andy Warhol, in which he said that in the olden days, if you saw someone who looked like your absolute sexual fantasy made flesh – a cowboy, say – he probably was just that. But ever since the advents of both irony and personal growth, there's no way of knowing whether the person who LOOKS like your absolute sexual fantasy is indeed that, or just doing it as a joke. Or even more interestingly, is dressed up as his or her OWN absolute sexual fantasy, like in *Midnight Cowboy*.

Similarly, though I thought I WANTED Mickey, I think it far more probable that I wanted to be LIKE him. His big battered face seemed more beautiful to me than any smoothie pin-up's, and I really admired the way he had totally let himself go. He wasn't anything like a gangster, as the poor deluded fool seemed to believe, but he was a bit like an old boxer, one who'd seen his dreams smashed to pieces shortly after his nose. I was awestruck at the amount of abuse his big burnt-out old body could take, and I SO wanted to be like him. (And now I am!) He made being one of the walking wounded look like a state of grace. All this and sadism too! It was hard to keep my mind on my Teazers with such pock-marked, paunchy pulchritude in the cubicle next door.

I understand that men are meant to 'chase' women, but I've never seen it that way. Because of their superior strength, it can look scary – there's always an element of stalking. On the other hand, I don't like nervous nellies who play hard to get, either. No, the best thing all round is just for a man to stand there looking sexy until a woman decides she wants to have sex with him. That way, there's the least possible margin for error. I may have been too young to vote and Mickey may have had one foot in the grave, but I knew which end was which. I took to strolling into his cubicle of an afternoon after downing half a shandy of Dutch courage and cunningly getting TP and Charlie – our limpet-like Plus Ones in the three-legged-race of office life – into a pointless argument over the merits of two equally useless bands, and staring moodily from him from the doorway. (I thought I looked moody; I probably just looked constipated.) He would look back at me, nervy yet resigned, then spread his hands and shrug – gorgeously Hebraic, it seemed to me, but wait for the twist in the cat'o'nine tails – and I would go and sit on his desk and place my long slender feet in their vertiginous heels on his lap. It wouldn't work these days, with my deformed size 8 plates of meat in their scuffed Ugg boots, but it was a good look at the time.

I Facebooked him the other day and said 'I basically stalked you, didn't I?' He answered back, 'I was so drunk that I didn't notice most of the time – maybe that was part of my charm.' It definitely was. He was so drunk so much of the time that it was easy to keep manoeuvring us into taxis together. We always seemed to be heading to the same show – the Sick Boys singing 'I Wanna Be Dead' or the Dead Boys singing 'I Wanna Be Sick' or some equally vile punk act – and it was a breeze to come over all ditsy when in fact I was calculating the night's direction to within an nth of an inch. 'I've just remembered!' I'd gasp audaciously at Tony, pushing the luckless Charlie towards him. 'You go on ahead – I'll go with Mickey!' From what little I remember, just about everyone was so variously stoned, speeding and sloshed out of their boxes back then that the ruse rarely needed a back-up plan.

Then it was bliss. I'd pour my darling doped-up

Mickey into a taxi, tell the driver to 'just drive' (a phrase so physically and fiscally – those expense accounts, back in the good old days of journalism! – exciting and exotic for a working-class kiddy whose parents had called a taxi exactly twice a year; to get to the station to catch the train to Butlin's, and on Christmas Day to get to my gran's) and sit and stare soulfully at him, till I got a drunken snog. Then he'd fiddle with his Sinex spray and mumble a bit and then address me, always respectfully, with a strange declaration, such as the aforementioned Virginia Woolf comparison or, even better, if rather sexist by today's standards, 'There are two sorts of women. Sisters – and pussy. And then there's YOU. Which makes three types of women...'

I knew it was a compliment – but to be honest, I would rather have been pussy.

Mickey was shacked up in some den of sin in Notting Hill with a girl called Ingrid von Essen, who HE thought looked like Brigitte Bardot but I thought favoured more Nico sawn off at the knees. She was foreign, icy and appeared incredibly self-possessed to a provincial 17-year-old. But when you're young, nothing stops you from having a bash at what you fancy. I knew a boy who worked at the same place as her, and through him I took to monitoring her business trips out of London with the same beady-eyed vigilance employed by the great – Jewish! – studio heads of the Golden Age of Hollywood following the menstrual cycles of their female stars, so as to know when they'd be best for their close-ups.

One day when I knew the Prussian foe was away, I got up early and decided to catch the old fool unawares; I've always been a morning person, whereas Mickey struck me as the sort of broken-down old war-horse who'd take quite a long time to come into consciousness each new golden dawn, fusting in his pit and wondering glumly why the 'Revolution' hadn't quite come off and all that jazz. Get in, get fucked, get out and get to work – he wouldn't see me coming. Heh heh!

Sniggering to myself like Muttley from *Wacky Races*, I squeezed into my Levis, poured myself into a white cap-sleeved T-shirt so tight that you could have probably calculated my age to the nearest calendar month by the rings around my nipples and jumped a train at the Angel to Westbourne Grove. Pausing only to steal a red apple from a greengrocer's, I walked up to Mickey's door and rang the bell. And there stood my demon lover, Sinex hanging from one nostril and his Isro apparently exploding. Talk about bed hair!

'Hello, Mickey.' I bit into the apple, he swallowed. 'Aren't you going to ask me in?'

'Yeah. Sure.' He stepped back as he always did for me, and I passed by him into the hallway. He pointed. 'Up there.'

Three steps to S&M heaven! 'Mickey?' I started up the stairs.

'Yeah?'

'You know this thing, sado-masochism?'

'Yeah.'

'Can you show me, please?'

Reader, he did.

1977 was a fun year for me, and definitely the most bruised year of my life thus far, even allowing for teeny tumbles as a tot. (Though it would not be the most bruised year of my life.) When I wasn't being whipped by my age-ing White Panther, I was getting myself into a tizzy at National Front counter-demonstrations, and spent many a pleasant Saturday afternoon full of righteous anger on the wrong side of a police horse.

My fellow *NME* inmates looked at me like I'd said I intended to ascend to Valhalla on a winged horse wearing deely-boppers when I announced in an editorial meeting that I intended to go to the big counter-demonstration in Lewisham that Saturday, and that I wanted to write about it for the paper. There was many a mumble of 'What's music got to do with politics?' from numbskulls who would shortly be sucking up to 'Red Wedge' like vacuum cleaners on heat, just as soon as some crooning moron had given politics the OK.

Sluggish spirals of cannabis smoke mingled with the sniggers of the nay-sayers, and I bristled indignantly. What a bunch of smelly, apolitical, idle hippies they truly were! 'If you go carrying pictures of Chairman Mao/You're not gonna make it with anyone anyhow!' Charlie piped up, quoting from the loathsome John Lennon song 'Rev-olution' which was probably written around the time our working-class hero was thinking of moving to Greece, under the notorious regime of the colonels, in order to pay less tax. He settled for New York and maintaining an unin-habited luxury apartment beneath the one he lived in, just to keep his wife's investment collection of fur coats at the right temperature, of course. What a hero worth quoting from, in the face of incipient fascism!

I shot CSM a withering look: I was buggered if HE was

going to tell me what made a person fuck-worthy or not! But I decided that I would appeal to him and Mickey – who was also sucking up lungfuls of evil weed and ignoring my piping plea to rally to the anti-fascist cause, the whip-wielding bed-wetter – as freedom-loving human beings, as opposed to a pair of numb-nuts who wouldn't know the National Front from the National Trust, they were so tucked-up-tidy with drugs and domesticity these days.

'Look, the National Front are against everything you two believe in.' Obviously, I meant they were Jews, but I'd realized – Yahweh knew why! – that some Jews were a bit touchy about being referred to as such. 'Just because you've had a bit of success, is that really an excuse to spend Saturday getting off your boxes when you could be showing solidarity with people who are getting picked on?'

Mickey made his excuses and left, the rotter – obviously SOMEONE had a pressing deadline for a pornographic short story, so the anti-fascist struggle could wait – but Charlie looked pensive, like a pigeon being patronizing. 'OK,' he finally agreed, 'I'll come.' I swear, I could hear the ghost of La Pasionaria getting all choked up with gratitude!

So with Charlie, Tony and *NME* photographer in tow, off we went to Lewisham that Saturday morning. There were lots of black people of all ages, lots of young white people and a few old white people. Next to me there was a very posh, very old man with a walking stick. As the National Front march came up and passed by us, he raised his stick and shouted at the top of his voice, 'JEW-BAITERS! DAMN JEW-BAITERS!' The young black and white people around him smiled at him lovingly; a Rastaman held his hand out for a high-five and the old posh man grasped it and shook it warmly. These days, of course, the Jew-baiters would be IN the anti-fascist crowd, as well as being heckled by it, due to all the half-wits now intent on sucking up to Islamofascism. Progress!

I broke ranks and ran at the NF column, shaking my right hand, limp at the wrist, in the international language of impotence, or was it wanking? I always forget. I was lividly young and beautiful, dressed head to toe in leather despite the heat of the mid-day sun, and I saw several NF men near to me go puce with petulance at the idea that such a pale, pretty girl could be on the other side. 'Wog meat!' went up the cry.

'That's right!' I yelled. 'And I love it!' I had never had sexual contact with a black man, but what the heck! – I looked back and saw Tony's anguish at my even pretending to have sex with any living organism. 'I love it, love it, LOVE IT!'

A bunch of NF numbskulls broke ranks and ran at me; I screamed like a girl and, attempting to run back to my mob, fell under a police horse. I got up quickly, dusted myself down, managed to shake off TP in the subsequent melee and went round Mickey's for a good whipping; the simple weekend pleasures of a wholesome 70s teenager, in less complicated times than these.

*

I started going to Left-wing bookshops. I hung around with the SWP. After reading our account of Lewisham, Paul Foot came up the *NME* to see Tony and me. I liked him. He wanted his photo taken with us and when I saw the Polaroid I commented skittishly 'Ooo, I look FAT!' (I was a size ten back then.) 'How could YOU ever look fat!' said the gallant Trot. O Mr Foot, had you but lived to see what happened to me!

Like a lot of people who become involved in politics, I was not as kind as I could have been to my nearest and dearest. Indeed, Tony's/the hippie chick's lament was being proved right! I remember at some point coming home for a rare visit to Bristol, and walking in on my dad – this strong, silent, Gary Cooper type – with tears running down his big Mount Rushmore face as he watched *Holocaust*, the television mini-series. 'The Jews,' he said. 'Girl, I never knew...'

'Well, good for you,' I snapped, before running up the stairs and snorting an indignant line of speed. 'Aren't you lucky!' I called back down the stairs for good measure. No two ways about it, I was always a bitch. BUT HOW COULD YOU GET TO MIDDLE-AGE WITHOUT KNOWING ABOUT THE SHOAH?

I wasn't kind to Tony either, snogging Mickey whenever we were all out in public and glorying in the facts that a) there wasn't a damn thing he could do about it as I'd made it clear I was never going to do the deed with him, TP, again and b) how much it hurt him. But he'd always come on like a right-heartbreaker – as opposed to my experience of him in the sack, where as I've mentioned he was more of a footstomper – boasting about all the foreign birds he'd had and how none of them could get enough of him, so I sort of tacked a righteous feminist angle to my basic bitch behaviour. He was being a total pain in the rear, moping about the kinderbunker more furiously than ever – the anti-fascist struggle, far from taking his mind off his own grievances as I'd hoped it might, had only served to bring out his self-dramatizing streak even further. He had taken to playing David Bowie's latest single 'Heroes' very loudly in the review room, with the door open, about once every thirty minutes. Then he'd mutter that Bowie probably wrote it about US, TP and JB, after reading our account of The Battle Of Lewisham! I'd laugh rudely, and he'd mutter darkly about 'ippies and sadists and fascists, casting meaningful looks at the Two Jews cubicle. Talk about a crazy mixed-up kid!

In an interview some decades later, Tony remembered us as becoming lovers – ICK! – again after Lewisham. I don't remember it that way AT ALL, bringing to mind what the very tall chorus girl is supposed to have said to the very short comedian who told her he wanted to have sex with her: 'If you do, and I hear about it, I'll be very cross!' Calling poor Jewish Mickey a fascist just because I fancied him was eye-crossingly illogical.

In another life I would come across this syndrome in one of my favourite books, Patrick Hamilton's *Hangover Square*, where Hamilton's perfectly nice and ordinary unrequited real-life love object, the actress Geraldine Fitzgerald, is evil-magicked into the Hitler-loving, fascist-fucking Netta Longdon, a very unamusing muse-hood which even made it into some of her obituaries. Of course, GF was no more a fascist than she was a fairy – but that she simply preferred someone else sexually wouldn't make a big enough story, and you wouldn't feel dignified getting all het up about it. But throw in a bit of fascism with your thwarted fuckery, and it's big drinks all round! I kicked myself for ever telling TP I was Jewish, thus adding to my many-hued bruises; he had chucked this bit of choice misinformation into his melodramatic mix, and it had made him even angrier. I could hardly turn round over a pint of snakebite at the Roxy and say conversationally 'Ooo, by the way, I'm not a Jew being whipped by a Fascist, I'm a Gentile being whipped by a Jew! So that's OK then?' I'd look a right mentalist.

Things came to a spectacular if squalid head shortly after my eighteenth birthday – as if being able to vote at last were not heady rush enough. There was a saying at the *NME* – 'When you've been on the road three times with Thin Lizzy, maybe it's time to quit.' I was luxuriating in my Jew-bruises, actually rubbing suntan oil into my arms to make them glow – believing that TP was away for the third time with Thin Lizzy and not having any inkling whatsoever about when to fold 'em – when in my erstwhile suitor walked.

El Tone stood there glowering at me like a maudlin matador in love with a particularly unreceptive bull, the best part of a year of lust and frustration fair radiating from him, my black and blue arms the red rag to his anger. Really, I mocked inwardly as I simpered sarcastically at him, we'd only slept together the once, and it had been about as much fun as watching sperm dry – what exactly WAS his problem? Of course I knew; it was me – I was the problem and the solution both. When this happens, we tend to call it love.

'What's that?' He pointed rudely.

'What's what?' I smirked.

'That. On your arms.'

'Oh,' I looked down at them, each in turn. 'THAT.' I looked him in the eye, and then as deliberately as an ear-piercing needle, I laughed.

That was it. HE WAS OFF! A moment later, a scream and a crash from the Two Jews' cubicle rang out and I ambled in to see my beloved Mickey sprawled inelegantly on the floor with blood on his mouth. I wondered if I should go to his aid, but he looked sort of...defeated, lying there with a bin as close to his head to be actually on it.

Instead, I turned to TP: 'Come on. Let's go home.'

Shortly afterwards, Tony invited his parents to meet me. They were brilliant people, and perceptive too; after I had left, his father said 'She's a lovely girl – but she's not Jewish.' When Tony confronted me with this possibility, I caved in quicker than you could say 'Pretendy Jewish Man from *Rolling Stone*.' Never mind, he informed me solemnly – he still wanted to marry me. In sheer embarrassment at being unmasked, I agreed.

We left London – throne of all my hopes and dreams – and moved to Billericay, Essex, a very small, quiet town where Tony had grown up. I was still a teenager. My short, thrilling life as a Jew was over. And the drought was back, with a vengeance.

(Postscript: I met Mickey years later in the 21st century, in my adopted hometown of Brighton, when I had become immensely rich and fat and was on my third and hopefully last marriage – and found out he wasn't a Jew at all! 'But if I had known you weren't a Jew, I'd never have let you whip me!' I wailed loudly across the table at the poor dying blighter in English's restaurant. Everyone stared, a waiter dropped one of those huge silver domey things, and I could all but hear the spirit of Vivien Leigh, once a regular at the august establishment, silently giving me her blessing for being such a mad bitch.)

FIVE

MEET THE PERVERTS

So when I was still a teenager, my first husband took me away from my beloved, mythical London and back to his hometown of Billericay, Essex; ostensibly because we couldn't afford to live in the capital, but really because he didn't want me running off with the first hot Jew who crossed my path. He was right, too. After five years he trusted me enough to let me go to a party in That There London – albeit accompanied by him – and I ran off with the first hot Jew who crossed my path.

The Hot Jew was Cosmo Landesman, a 29-year-old boulevardier who looked like a Chosen version of John Taylor from Duran Duran. Way back in the 1980s day, that is; recently, when he wrote a newspaper piece about going on date with a Jewish grandmother, I had to look twice to make out which one the Jewish grandmother was. But then, as my mirror bears mute witness each day, we all lose our charms in the end.

We met at a book launch at the Turf Club in Carlton House Terrace in the spring of 1984 – and truly, from the moment I saw him I was committing Thought Crimes left, right and especially centre. Though my old ball and chain was sitting so close to me you couldn't have slipped a condom between us, from the minute I saw the Hot Jew, everything faded away – like in *West Side Story*, when the star-crossed lovers meet at the dance in the gym.

In his book, *Starstruck: Fame, Failure, My Family And Me*, Mr Landesman remembers meeting me thus:

I saw a young woman sitting on a sofa who was all legs, pale skin, flaming-red lips, and was wrapped tight in a black bandage of a dress...She looked like a film noir beauty and had the strange, nervy manner of a shy alien.

I've always loved the song 'I Remember It Well' sung by the two old duffers in *Gigi*, and no doubt time, the great vandal, has been equally free in his ruffian ways with both myself and my second husband, memory-wise. But as I recall, it wasn't I who behaved like a strange, nervy alien. Because although the Turf Club may have been a million miles from the Roxy, I felt strangely at ease there – the stylized blankness of the revellers and the paintings of beasts on the wall made one feel utterly at home in one's Englishness. Whereas this vision staring at me from across the room – all legs, olive skin, bug-eyes and sharp suit – was so obviously The Other as to be laughable – if I weren't already drooling with lust. I wiped my mouth with a delicate pinky, gave a tinkly laugh at something dreary some dullard had said, and wondered who the Hot Jew was.

I didn't have long to wait. The HJ walked across the room with all the sheer molten focus of a Slinky on heat.

Amazingly, the vision perched on the arm of my sofa; my eyes widened – men had been fed laxatives for less! I stole a look at TP but he was busy being all vivacious and Cockney for some braying types. Only the prospect of showing off, I had learned, could take his mind off of his mission of acting as my bespoke guard dog for the rest of my days. As I had recently been offered a column at the *Sunday Times* while he had failed to even get an interview for the post of editor of *Stamp Collecting Monthly* – true! – he had taken to trumping up himself big-time whenever there were media-ocrities within sniffing distance.

I smiled encouragingly at the HJ. It stared back, eyes on stalks, and blurted, 'I'm Cosmo Landesman.'

What a lovely name – Jew in one! 'Oh, I've heard of you,' I said warmly. He looked surprised and gratified. 'Yes, you're the son of that famous open marriage. I read about it in *Cosmopolitan* when I was a little girl.'

He looked sad, but gamely attempted to recover his footing. 'Do you like men in suits?'

'Why...yes,' I replied, perplexed.

'Do you think young people have stopped reading?'

'Um...no.'

'What is the book on your bedside table?'

I laughed. 'I don't have a bedside table! What am I, FIFTY?'

The ice was broken, and I was falling through it, straight into the undertow of love.

*

As I grew to know him – and to love him, though the two experiences did not make natural bedfellows; neither, come to that, did we, apart from both being sex maniacs – I would discover that Mr Landesman was, as lazy travel writers often say of countries, a creature of contrasts. He was immensely sociable, but extremely self-loathing. This meant that he would go to a real shed load of literary parties, but then once he was at the parties he would feel unworthy of talking to the wide range of personality disorders who passed as famous writers. He used to perform a routine for me after we were married and I had sent him off to yet another media scrum by himself, which he described nicely in *Starstruck*:

> *I stand and munch, and then I move on with a drink in my hand. I look like a man who is scanning the room for an imaginary friend. I've made him up because I don't want to look like I don't know anyone here, so I keep moving....it's funny, when you're young you think how great it would be to be an Invisible Man – and then you grow up and go to parties with famous people and you realize that you ARE the invisible man and it's not so great after all....I spot another guy with a drink, pushing his way through the crowd with an air of purpose, as though he's looking for a friend. He looks at me, I look at him. He knows that I know his secret: he's the other Lonely Guy in the room.*

I could never understand this way of thinking – I am at my least lonely when I am alone, even though I love company and in my old age have become quite the convivialist. It strikes me as verging on the mentally unbalanced to seek self-esteem through the approval of others. But, I realized that first night I met poor Mr Landesman, such was the unbearably light burden of this modern-day Wandering Jew, forever bouncing between nightclubs and canapés in his search for significance. Talk about looking for love in all the wrong places.

(We were temperamentally very different. Cosmo was a moaning pessimist – a family nickname was 'Eeyore' – while I was an enthusiastic optimist, rather like Tigger. This difference was crystallised for me in 1986, two years into our marriage, when we saw a late night discussion programme on TV, chaired by Michael Ignatieff. It was called *The Tough And The Tender: Modernity And Its Discontents* and featured the philosophers Ernest Gellner (tough: a gorgeous scrappy old Jew) and Charles Taylor (tender, the big Jessie) going at it hammer and tongs while Ignatieff ducked whistling missiles in the middle. Basically, Gellner thought that we lived in the best of all possible times and should relish the instability of modern life because of the possibility of great progress and freedom; Taylor, the old worry wart, harped on with various variations of the eternal mum-nag of Things Not Being What They Used To Be. Cosmo and I immediately picked our sides and set up a sort of echo chamber in our red bedroom as we watched the debate avidly. I've never been averse to a low blow, to be honest, and when I'd finally had enough of Cosmo bleating on about how great things were in medieval times when everybody knew their place – sorry, 'was certain of their role' – I said to him, 'Well, it's a good job we're NOT in medieval times, or you'd be chasing a chicken around a shtetl somewhere and being whipped by Cossacks, instead of in bed with a hot piece of shiksa ass like me!' Undeterred, he began to plan a Fitzgeraldesque novel called *The Tough And The Tender* about a Jewish/ Gentile couple called Nathan and Stella – no prizes! – and their media mates. I was in absolute stitches when I saw in the synopsis that my character, Stella, eventually committed suicide by chucking herself off Brighton Pier! But a) I'm a really good swimmer and b) I'm so not the suicidal type, so it was far more likely that Nathan/Cosmo would have jumped, the neurotic numpty. Though dead women do seem to be a motif of art, past and present – or maybe it was just wishful thinking.)

Still, love was what we appeared to have found. We embarked on an affair, and suffice it to say (I've always wanted to write that!) that everything I had imagined in my deepest, darkest teenage dreams about Jews and sex was apparently true. After a few months of meeting in Mr Landesman's World's End digs for sex each week, I found myself rudely shaken awake by my husband after I had dropped off on the sofa one night.

'WHAT DID YOU SAY?' TP yelled.

'I don't know – what DID I say?' I blurred.

'You said "Cosmo – give it to me"!' TP roared. It sounded so funny in his butch Essex bellow that I couldn't help laughing. Under cover of my hilarity, I thought quickly. Reaching out a hand to where *Cosmopolitan* magazine lay on the floor (thank goodness it wasn't *Fur & Feather*!) I waved it playfully in his face. 'Mission accomplished! I'll say please next time...'

Nevertheless, I was taken aback by my sex-crazed

somnambulist slip-up, and rang my HJ as soon as the coast was clear. 'I can't stay here anymore. I want to come away with you.'

HJ didn't miss a beat. 'I want that too. Let me ring you back.' Within five minutes he'd arranged for us to go to ground at another HJ's place, some crazy space-age millionaire's place in Hampstead. I kissed my four-year-old son goodbye, told my husband I was going to visit my mum, and ran away, yet again.

Could I have behaved better? Undoubtedly. Am I glad I left? Unconditionally.

*

The millionaire HJ's place was lush, no doubt about it. But it wasn't JEWISH. It could just as easily have belonged to an illiterate footballer, an Arab potentate or one of those superior robots off the SMASH adverts.

'Let's go and stay with your parents!' I suggested. I'd already met his mother and his brother during our affair – his mother had written a poem about me and his brother had wondered if I could get his band reviewed in the *NME*, so I knew what a bunch of wannabes I was hooking up with.

Cosmo looked pained. 'You sure you wanna? You know Fran and Jay are crazy.'

'They're Jewish – they're NEUROTIC,' I corrected him. 'Like in Philip Roth books!'

Frankly, I could have told Cosmo I wanted to go and live in a maisonette on Mars at that point in our relationship and he would have called a cab and mixed me a martini while we waited. 'O.K! So long as you can handle a pair of fame-crazed ageing Jews who are gonna think all their Christmases have come at once...'

'Hannukahs,' I corrected.

He gave me an old-fashioned look. 'OK. You asked for it!'

Despite my HJ's warning, I was not prepared for how thoroughly un-Jewish – by my naïve standards – his parents were. Sure, I had read about their open marriage when I was a kiddy in Bristol, and thrilled to its outlandish outlawness, the very antithesis of my parents' forsaking-all-others faithfulness. But then I expected Jews to be keener on sex than other people – that was part of the attraction. When she was interviewed at the age of 75 about her 'ménage à trois', Fran was comically offended by the suggestion that only one other person had been involved. 'A "ménage à trois" implies some kind of fidelity,' she huffed. 'It wasn't just one other person. It was a lot of people.' Not so much Guess Who's Coming To Dinner, more Guess Who's Coming To Do You.

What I wasn't prepared for, on the other hand, was the sheer non-sexual aspect of filth that featured strongly in the Landesman family home. In 1993, Cosmo's father reminisced to the *Independent* about our brief lodging there:

Their move into our north London house was temporary; the only space available was an old workroom that had been turned into a storage area for broken things. Although it overlooked the garden, the view was hidden by a tangle of ivy. Bars across the window gave it a jail-like atmosphere, perfect for the new prisoners of love. Fran and I felt like the homo-sexual couple in La Cage aux Folles *who try to clean up their act when the son brings his girlfriend home for a visit. Cosmo had already warned us that Julie knew all about us. She hated hippies, ex-hippies, food freaks, open marriages and, worst of all, old people. The only thing she liked about us was that we were Jewish.*

The first sour note was her introducing white bread into the house. Cosmo, who hadn't seen white bread since puberty, thought it was exotic. Our first dinner with them was almost a success. We got a rave review from Cosmo on the artichokes but not from Julie, who had never seen one before and who said it looked nasty.

Sadly, 'nasty' was a word which could have been applied to many aspects of the Landesman lair in the Angel, Islington, a seven-storey Georgian house which had been going for a song in the Sixties and had gone for a Burton long since. I wasn't expecting a Bohemian type like Fran to be polishing the menorahs, baking lokshen pudding and exclaiming 'Oy! My lovely kinder!' all hours of the day. But, being of humble origins, I was used to a clean house. Cleanliness is next to Godliness indeed, and this bunch of flea-ridden atheists were living, scratching proof of the converse.

I don't generally like beards on men – on bread, I find them even less appealing. So my first reaction on finding a loaf in the Landesman kitchen bearing a burden which it would have wearied ZZ Top to wear between them was to throw it in the rubbish when I came across it one day while helpfully cleaning up the frankly Skid Row – Death Row, even – level kitchen. I went back to bed with my HJ and thought no more about it until a high-pitched keening from the kitchen disturbed our post-coital slumber.

'Who's been in my fucking kitchen? Where's my freaking bread?' It was Fran, fresh up from her six-hour cannabis-clouded afternoon nap and not a happy hippie AT ALL.

I scrambled up, pulled on my IDF T-shirt and ran quickly upstairs to confess to the dreadful sin of cleanliness.

'Sorry Fran, it was me – it had awful sort of HAIR growing out of it...'

'Hey, sheweetheart, that's when it gets GOOD!' Jay, the loony old lounge lizard, had oiled up behind me soundlessly – only he could wring a double entendre out of some mouldy old dough. If Cosmo was a Jewish Sex Dream come true, you could see where he got it from. His dad had recently acquired both his senior citizen's bus pass and a twenty-something girlfriend: a well-spoken, quite boring, attractive gamine who worked in the press office for the Girl Guides and was thus known as 'Gigi.' It was the first time I had come across a gerontophile since I myself had dallied with the thirty-something Mick Farren as a teenager, and I was both repelled and fascinated by their set-up. Cosmo, who was older than her, was just plain embarrassed. And probably envious, looking back.

Fran, who at 57 was eight years younger than Jay, was

considered by both father and son to be invalided out of the sexual arena by virtue of old age, and now lived in a state of celibacy, cooking dinner for Gigi who joined the family to 'dine' – using the word loosely – most nights. Even in my twenties this struck me as rank hypocrisy – there's no hypocrite like a hipster, in my experience – and it must have had some influence on the foul mood she spent much of her time in. That and the endless amount of tofu and mung beans she was supposed to work miracles with. I got the impression that a part of her would just liked to have kicked back and eaten cake, but Jay was the mad mastermind behind the macrobiotic kick. Years back, when Cosmo was a kiddy and his parents' open marriage was at its slaggy heights, his father had threatened his mother with divorce when he surprised her on holiday eating an ice lolly. Now that she had hobbled off the perving pitch for an early bath (alone), their positions were even more unequal. Once more, I reflected that hippies beat Tories every time when it came to sexism.

While Fran was stuck at home sweating over the evil-smelling ingredients she was allowed to use, Jay was out at the newly-opened Groucho Club inhaling vast quantities of martinis and chatting up young chicks – a bit of a sitcom-style generation-gap laff-opp, as this was also where Cosmo, myself and our gang liked to hang out of an evening. If Cosmo thought he had been embarrassed by his dad when he took to turning up at Open Days at Cosmo's rough comprehensive school wearing a kaftan, those were fast shaping up to be the happiest days of his life now that Jay – who had spent a lifetime chasing celebrities, and celebrity – had a live one living under his roof. Me. I was baffled – I mean, the Landesmans had hung out with Lenny Bruce, Jack Kerouac and the Beatles in their magic mushroom salad days, and I was just some hack from the pop press who'd been lucky enough to land a cushy billet in Fleet Street.

Cosmo wrote about it in *Starstruck*:

It was as if Jay had won the pools. He couldn't wait to tell everyone the good news. In the early days of our marriage, he underwent a personality transformation, and from being my father became this other creature: Julie Burchill's Father-In-Law.

I assumed that he would soon calm down once the novelty wore off, but his Julie mania only grew worse. The first time it really angered me was when I attended a Labour Party rally with Julie, who was then political correspondent of the Mail On Sunday. *We arrived at the venue and were met by a PR who told us of a strange encounter with an American man claiming to be Julie Burchill's father-in-law and demanding to be let in.*

I didn't mind this much at all – it was a small price to pay for the privilege of being allowed to MARRY INTO A JEWISH FAMILY, no matter how oddball. 'Mrs LANDESMAN,' I would always enunciate preciously over the phone, 'L-A-N-D-E-S-M-A-N. Land Is Man!' I revelled in my new role as a Jewish wife. When we moved into a mansion block in Southampton Row, we lived next door to an Indian family. One day, I found a crude swastika etched into the communal wall between our two front doors. I stood looking at it for quite a while, torn between pride and revulsion. When the Indian lady next door came out, I was still looking at it. 'Excuse me,' I mused, 'but do you think this is OUR swastika – or is it yours?'

As the 80s rolled on, I failed at each Hebraic hurdle. When Cosmo and I had a baby, Jack, I booked the mohel to come to the hospital – then made a fool of myself crying when he arrived, begging him to 'go away and please don't hurt my baby!' I could appreciate as well as any other Gentile day-tripper the benefits of circumcision in the male – beauty, lack of various cancers – but when it came to my baby having part of his cock cut off, I recoiled with all the cosmopolitan ennui of a Thomas Hardy heroine.

Also, my in-laws taught me that Jews could be human – all too human. I'll never forget listening to Fran tell a story about how, as a teenager in Connecticut, she had been barred from a country club just for being a Jew. I was making the usual sympathetic faces that any civilized human being would make, until I heard her yell 'AND I'VE HATED BEING A FUCKING JEW EVER SINCE!' Snapped into action, I challenged 'But Fran – THEY were in the wrong, not you!' She shot back 'As long as the Jews believe they're CHOSEN – they asked for it. They ASKED to be gassed!'

There's no answer to that. I've tried to explain to numerous people – some hysterical, like my dead Jewish mother-in-law, some in their right minds, like my living Gentile husband – what CHOSEN means. It DOESN'T mean that the Jews were picked out and put above everybody else. It means that they were TOLD first. Then everybody else had a chance to listen. If they chose not to listen, it's not the fault of the Jews.

*

Regrettably, it was one Jew's fault that my marriage to him ended. In an interview with the *Jewish Chronicle*, Mr Landesman spoke thus:

> *'I loved being married to Julie. To have a wife who makes you laugh so much you can't breathe is a wonderful thing. I'll tell you one thing, mate, it wasn't boring.'*
>
> *Burchill is famously philo-semitic. Did Landesman have anything to do with that? 'Her love of Jews and things Jewish was there before she met me. She always said she wanted to marry a Jew. I guess I was just the right Jew in the right place.'*

The way I look at it, if he had been nicer, I might have been tempted to stay with him – because I DID love him – but then I'd never have met my third husband, Daniel, who has brought me such happiness for the past 18 years; longer than both my other marriages put together.

It's amazing what you can do to people in the name of love, and what you can say about them in the name of friendship, and they're meant to put up with it. Even leaving Daniel aside, I've never regretted leaving my fast media life in London for my somewhat slower seaside life, and one of the reasons is that, to put it bluntly, my Brighton friends, male and female, look out for me. They may be a bunch of gypsies, tramps and thieves compared to my

Oxbridge Double First best friends from my London life – but they've got soul. Ironic looking the other way? Postmodern turning the other cheek? Not a chance in hell!

SIX

OFF MY FACE IN THE PROMISED LAND

At some point in their lives, every philo-Semite must ask themselves a question. And by the way, I'm talking SERIOUS philo-Semites here – not those pussies who go for the small stuff. *Jewish Mother Of The Year*! my friends kept reminding me for a few weeks in 2012. 'I bet you'll be watching THAT! And *Jews At Ten*! And *Friday Night Dinner*! And that new sit-com where he marries a Jewish girl and takes her up North – Hebburn!' Over a lovely plate of chopped liver, pastrami and lox, no doubt, all washed down by copious draughts of chicken soup, while capering about to klezmer music?

But strange to say, I saw none of them. Neither have I ever watched *Curb Your Enthusiasm*. I positively LOATHE Woody Allen. I despise bagels. And I don't really have much time for families. Ever extreme, I have simply avoided the usual half-hearted gestures towards Jew-fancying, and cut straight to the chase. The things I love about the Jews are the REAL things about them, the things that make lots of people uncomfortable and uncomprehending – their religion, their language and their ancient, reclaimed country. The small stuff – food, humour – I can take or leave.

The question is this – what came first, the Jew or the Israeli? And whom do you love best? Of course, like I do, you can choose both; you can admire certain Jews for their bookishness and sensitivity while also seeing that it's sort of nice for other Jews to get a chance at being big dumb jocks striding around in the shameless sunshine of their own country after all those centuries of scurrying around dependent on the goodwill of some hulking, pallid half-wits not fit to lick their kippahs. But it was to be many years into my life as a philo-Semite that I would experience the miracle of modern Israel at first hand. And then, frankly, I was so drunk a lot of the time I was there that I don't remember as much about it as I should.

Around the turn of the century (I've always wanted to write that – instant gravitas) I took on a part-time cleaner because I had acquired a big house on the South Coast with six bedrooms – bought solely for the outdoor swimming pool: half-Olympic size! – and thought I should make some sort of pretence at being a grown-up. I've never been good with 'help' – I'm too working-class, too generous and too freaking bright not to see the inherent hilarity of one person cleaning up after another. My mum had been a cleaner at various times, and the idea of myself as some born-again Lady Muck overseeing a shivering tweeny – 'You've missed a bit!' – struck me as being so drag-queeny as to be absolutely un-doable with a straight face.

In London, I had occasionally used a babysitting service for my son Jack which recruited mostly young black

African primary school teachers, and while I had no problem leaving these exemplary young women in my flat of
an evening with a half-bottle of champagne, a box of Pre-
stat choccies and a twenty-pound tip when I got in, it was
a bridge too far when I started asking the same agency
to send the occasional cleaner round and the same exemplary type of young black African woman started turning
up. I was SO not going to sit around being cleaned for by
a black person! So I'd put some Anita Baker on the boom-
box, clean along with them – talk about neither use nor
ornament – and pay them twice the going rate.

But I STILL couldn't get used to the idea of black people working for white ones. ('Baby, you're so not a Jew –
they have no problem with it,' pointed out Cosmo helpfully. He had practically been raised by a black woman,
the wonderfully-named Alfie Clay, during the first decade
of his life in St Louis, Missouri, while his parents devoted
themselves to the more pressing tasks of running nightclubs and shagging around.)

So I rang up the agency; 'Hello, it's Mrs Landesman.
Could you please, I mean is there any way, umm is it possible – that you could stop sending black girls –'

Bang went the receiver at the other end – totally cutting off the rest of the sentence, which was going to be
along the lines of '– to clean for me, but please continue to
send them over to sit with the dearest person in the world
to me while I'm out.' I had set out with love for humanity, and ended up being struck off as a racist. Me – who
proudly shared a swastika with an Indian family!

But I figured I'd persevere now that I had a big house
to look after – and let's face it, Brighton's a lot whiter than

London, so there was less scope for racial embarrassment. They sent a couple of nice Caucasian cleaners, and they and I got along fine because the house was big enough that I could keep out of their way without coming over all audience-participatory. Then – third time lucky – they sent Nadia.

Her father had been a Serb, her mother an Italian and she herself born and bred in Yorkshire; she seemed to me like an ambulatory archive of these stereotypical national and regional types – proud, fiery and forthright. And the first time she came to work for me, I came into the room to find her touching an Israeli flag on my wall with a delicacy which was almost reverent. She turned to smile at me with real radiance: 'I love the Jews!'

Well, what COULD I do? I pulled out the vacuum cleaner by its plug, pulled a gramme of cocaine from my pocket and shook it in her face: 'Worker's playtime?' And so it was that I found one of my life's greatest companions and fellow philo-Semites. It would have probably been even more enjoyable if we hadn't been two half-crazy drunkards capable of starting a fight in an empty, locked room – but as it was, it was pretty damn good.

*

By 2004 I was working for the *Times*, and was still something of a blue-eyed girl at this stage in my career, the Thunderer having taken me from the *Guardian* and paid handsomely for the privilege. Shortly before I left the *Guardian*, I wrote the following:

If there is one issue that has made me feel less loyal

to my newspaper over the past year, it has been what I, as a non-Jew, perceive to be a quite striking bias against the state of Israel. Which, for all its faults, is the only country in that barren region that you or I, or any feminist, atheist, homosexual or trade unionist, could bear to live under. I find this hard to accept because, crucially, I don't swallow the modern liberal line that anti-Zionism is entirely different from anti-semitism; the first good, the other bad. Judeophobia is a shape-shifting virus, as opposed to the straightforward stereotypical prejudice applied to other groups (Irish stupid, Japanese cruel, Germans humourless, etc). Jews historically have been blamed for everything we might disapprove of: they can be rabid revolutionaries, responsible for the might of the late Soviet empire, and the greediest of fat cats, enslaving the planet to the demands of international high finance. They are insular, cliquey and clannish, yet they worm their way into the highest positions of power in their adopted countries, changing their names and marrying Gentile women. They collectively possess a huge, slippery wealth that knows no boundaries – yet Israel is said to be an impoverished, lame-duck state, bleeding the West dry.

If you take into account the theory that Jews are responsible for everything nasty in the history of the

world, and also the recent EU survey that found 60%
of Europeans believe Israel is the biggest threat to
peace in the world today (hmm, I must have missed
all those rabbis telling their flocks to go out with
bombs strapped to their bodies and blow up the near-
est mosque), it's a short jump to reckoning that it was
obviously a bloody good thing that the Nazis got rid
of six million of the buggers. Perhaps this is why sales
of Mein Kampf *are so buoyant, from the Middle East-*
ern bazaars unto the Edgware Road, and why The
Protocols of The Elders of Zion *could be found for sale*
at the recent Anti-racism Congress in Durban.

To add insult to injury, the *Guardian* had also recently run
an opinion piece by none other than Osama bin Laden –
and the thought of being bed-mates with this arch anti-
Semite was too much for even my sexually flexible sensi-
bility. When they told me that I could not have an annual
raise in salary, but that the paper would buy me a sofa
instead, I saw red – I bet they didn't offer a skanky bit of
soft furnishing to classy old Polly Toynbee! Proffering a
sofa as opposed to actual money was very close to saying
'Listen, you're not like the rest of our writers – you didn't
even go to university, FFS, you peasant! And we know you
just lie around stuffing chocs all day. Take this "settee", as
I believe you oiks call it, and be grateful!'

So when the *Times* came calling, I promptly skedad-
dled, especially pleased when they did an unprecedented
thing and signed me up for a whopping three years. I felt a
bit like a Premier-league footballer – which is to say, I was

drunk and AWOL a great deal of the time and totally took my eye off the ball. Before long, the Thunderer would offer me the rest of my contract money to go away and not come back. But in the early days, it struck me that now I was free of an anti-Israel paper and working for a more civilized publication – and that I might actually bite the bullet, take the plunge and GO TO ISRAEL, ALL EXPENSES PAID!

Of course, I would take Nadia with me. We had been on holiday together before, to Lanzarote, where Nadia had somehow managed to book us into a hotel which was full of Germans – not just a few Germans, but literally everyone apart from us; two hard-core philo-Semites, one with Serbian blood! It was a nightmare; the German hausfraus tutted and winced as we – the only unaccompanied women there – slung our middle-aged racks around and chaindrank lurid blue cocktails poolside, and we in turn despised them for their habit of living up to the tragic German cliché about getting up at 5 AM in order to bag the best sun loungers. One morning, after an impromptu champagne breakfast, Nadia lost her temper and threw a pair of Bavarian towels into the pool; I goggled and giggled, delighted and amazed to have a friend even badder and more bolshy than me, and we promptly took up occupancy on the liberated loungers. Ten minutes later, a generic German – shorts, glasses, no apparent penis – came out, walked over to us and narrowed his eyes: 'Ah, I see you have brought your manners with you from the island!' he hissed.

FROM THE ISLAND! YOUR MANNERS! Well, it was a red rag – and Nadia, jumping up from her lounger, proceeded to do a very good impression of a pretty blonde bull barnstorming through a brief history of Europe circa 1933 to 1945. 'And don't EVER forget that Hitler was ELECTED!' she finished triumphantly as the German beat a hasty retreat. After that, our name was mud, and we tended to stay in our room of an evening, talking about how much we loved the Jews while the Krauts cavorted to the strains of an oompah band beneath our balcony. One evening, we watched in disbelief as 9/11 took place on our hotel room TV screen. It was probably our imagination, but the Germans seemed to frolic with extra enthusiasm that night.

We became a Gang of Two, behaving more like fourteen-year-olds than fortysomethings. And our love of the Jews and Israel was the backbone which prevented this friendship from being simply about getting wasted and wasting time. When I asked Nadia to come to Israel with me, an assignment I would write up for the *Times*, she burst into tears. I felt like I had asked her to gay-marry me. And as with many a marriage, it would not only start with tears, but end in them too.

*

Between 2004 and 2010, Nadia and I would visit Israel four times. The first time, because we had a guide and I was writing it up as an assignment from the *Times*, it was relatively civilized. The second time we met up with some Jewish mates from England and had a really lively time. The third time I hurt my leg falling over drunk the first night, the Icelandic volcano went off, and we were stuck by a swimming pool in Eilat for two weeks, drinking our body weight in Israeli wine. The last time, I'm afraid to say, is just a drunken blur. To be honest, all the visits are, to some extent. But blurs punctuated by the searing, soaring beauty of Israel.

I have friends, fellow philo-Semites such as my friend Chas Newkey-Burden, who go to Israel with excellent organizations such as Stand With Us and do lovely stuff like go to markets with groups of volunteers and help elderly shoppers carry their bags home, and plant trees in the Aminadav forest outside Jerusalem. And wholesome stuff, like cycling and hiking in the Judaean desert. And proper political stuff, like having tea with Gilad Shalit's family at their protest tent, touring the security fence, meeting IDF spokesmen and going to the Knesset, where he had a go at MKs for not looking after the Gush Katif expellees.

I wish I could look back and be similarly proud of what I've contributed to the well-being of the country I admire above all others, but sadly my only outstanding contribution has been to those Israelis holding a liquor licence. (Oh, and a LOT of big tips. I love being a big tipper – a taxi driver once told me that the best tippers were 'tarts, Jews and journalists' – one of the few occasions I've felt tempted to sit down and do a Venn diagram of myself.) So my list would read more like 'Got drunk at Mike's Place in Tel Aviv. Got drunk over breakfast at Café Café in Eilat. Got drunk at the King David Hotel in Jerusalem.' That sort of thing.

But the 2004 trip was amazing – not a word I use loosely. Even before your baggage goes through airport X-ray machines so huge that it would be possible for a standing adult, barely stooping, to walk through one, everything about going to Israel is larger than life, which is strange considering that it's a country the size of Wales. Everything from the clothes you need to pack – not many, nothing warm, because it's always hot and always informal unless you plan to hang around some neurotic, misogynistic Muslim/Catholic 'Holy Place', in which case, COVER YOURSELF YOU FILTHY DAUGHTER OF A WHORE! – to the reaction you get from your friends – OH NO, YOU'RE GOING TO DIEEEEEE! – is Not Normal. But that feeling ended, for me, the minute I was settled on the El Al aircraft. Looking around at my fellow passengers, in their various skullcaps, side-curls and crop-tops, I felt an eerie sense of calm, so different from the irritation, nerves and boredom that air travel usually provokes. My favourite bit of the King James Bible, verse 16, Chapter 1 of The Book of Ruth, came back to me, triumphantly this time after a lifetime of aloneness: 'Intreat me not to leave thee, or to return from following after thee; for whither thou goest, I will go; and where thou lodgest, I will lodge; thy people shall be my people, and thy God my God.'

To be among them, but not of them; to 'pass', of all the outrageous things, when one of the stewardesses (minimal make-up, stern slacks; Israeli girls make the rest of us, even Oriental women, look like inappropriate drag queens, but somehow you can't hate them because they're beautiful as they don't mean to be) speaks to me in Hebrew! I can't get over this – it's what I've been waiting for since I was 14! – but my face falls a little when snub-nosed, baby-blonde Nadia is similarly spoken to; no one could mistake her for one. Bitch. And this is the first of many sad lessons

I learn in Israel – that because of the terrible fall-off in tourism since the Intifada, Israelis presume that they have no friends abroad any more. They simply presume that every person on an Israeli plane, or in an Israeli hotel, is an Israeli.

Then a well-groomed lady – the stereotypical curious, kind, clichéd Sadie – who'd been utilizing the aisles for a bit of a pry looked at me, did a double-take, and pronounced loudly 'O! It's Julie Burchill!' Other ladies came to look at me and shake my hand. If I had been made of matzo at that glorious moment, I would have eaten myself. I was still just about in the outer suburbs of my beauty then; one of the ladies asked me if I was married, and showed me a photograph of her handsome, single son. I thought of that line from F. Scott Fitzgerald's essay *Early Success*:

...when the fulfilled future and the wistful past were mingled in a single gorgeous moment – when life was literally a dream.

Don't ever travel Business Class to Israel, if you can help it. Yes, you'll feel like the Big I Am. But you just won't get the sheer oomph! of what Israel is. The crop-topped teenage girls blowing bubblegum next to prayer-shawled Haredim. The soft-hearted gangsters holding the toilet doors open for the cold-eyed grandmas. The Russian blondes and the Mizrahi brunettes. And the way everyone cheers when the plane touches down in the Promised Land. Not the usual drunken huzzah but the sheer molten joy of a people living who might well have never been born had all gone to monstrous plan just a while back. No, in Business Class you get only bliss. And bliss is a poor thing, compared to Israel.

The first night we were there, Nadia and I checked into the David's Citadel hotel in Jerusalem, dropped our bags on the floor – and ran out, holding hands and screaming, to the first bar we could find, a karaoke joint full of beautiful Ethopians. We did shot after shot but we couldn't get drunk – we were too high already. We took it in turns to say, 'We're in Israel...' It remains one of the strangest and most beautiful non-sex nights of my life.

Though I find Jerusalem the saddest, scariest place on earth, a trip to Israel that doesn't include it feels hollow somehow. It's the whole point of everything, the reason Israel exists, no matter how much that may be obscured by the smorgasbord of sunshine and sexiness. Jerusalem is about the altogether serious business of religion; here I would at last find Zionists whose conviction was as unabashed as mine – busloads of black Christians from the USA who called me 'sister' when we spoke. There would be a Jerusalem without Tel Aviv or Eilat – but there wouldn't be a Tel Aviv or an Eilat without Jerusalem. It is simply the most splendid and most sorrowful place I've ever seen. But steer clear of the King David Hotel – despite its obvious beauty, the heavy weight of history can make checking in feel like volunteering to be walled up in a mausoleum. Last time I was there, small birds had a habit of getting in through the windows and fluttering helplessly along the corridors, adding to the impression of the hotel as a unsafe haven for unquiet souls.

The next morning, our guide came to take us to Yad Vashem, the huge and, it must be said, beautiful memorial to the genocide of the European Jews in the first half of the 20th century. I won't try to describe it here; enough to say that we arrived at 9am and didn't feel able to leave until 1pm. Our guide spoke to us softly after about three hours: 'Julie, Nadia. I hate to have to say this. But we must go soon.' We were uncontrollable in our grief; every time we thought we could move on, one of us would utter a cry of anguish and dart back into the darkness of the halls. When were finally done, we sat in the Israeli sun and Nadia said, 'Thank goodness we've always loved them. Imagine being one of those people who talk trash about them. And then seeing THAT. And knowing that the way you think helped create that.'

I remember so much about that first trip, nearly a decade ago now. The dolphins free to come and go in at the dolphinarium in Eilat – the only such set-up I've ever come across. Our guide crying one night at dinner and saying 'BUT WHAT IF IT HAPPENS AGAIN?' The walk along the Tel Aviv seafront to Jaffa. The way I suddenly 'got' the whole Bauhaus thing; the buildings look so grim when you see them in the European rain, and so joyful when you see them in the Israeli sunshine, More than four thousand Bauhaus buildings built in the 1930s by refugee German Jewish architects make up the White City quarter in Tel Aviv – as though a racial memory inspired the scattered Jews of Europe to create buildings which would only become beautiful when born again in the historic Hebrew homeland. The way the heartbreakingly young security guards ask you 'Do you have a gun?' plainly and politely at the airports and shopfronts which, like the fact that every Israeli baby – Jew, Christian and Muslim – goes home from hospital with a tiny gas mask, makes you aware each time exactly what these people deal with, with such grace under pressure, day after day.

It's a good idea to have a guide – they drive you around and keep you on the straight and narrow in more ways than one. But after our first visit, partly because of the small size of Israel – there's only one major thing wrong with the country, in my opinion, and that's that it could use being a bit bigger – and partly because of the huge size of our joint self-esteem, we figured we could do it just as well by ourselves. Predictably, taking into account that our idea of fun was getting smashed as soon as possible in the day and staying that way as long as we could manage, subsequent visits were nowhere near as enlightening and vivifying as the first. Still, so many memories; I'm not a big fan of the word 'bittersweet', but that's what they probably are – a big old bouquet of bittersweet coulda-shoulda-wouldas.

On our second visit we did the Tel Aviv-Jerusalem tour again, and it was still great, if somewhat more hungover than the officially guided original.

The third time, jaded and lazy, we aimed for a week in Eilat – Israel's only resort city – in April 2010. But then the Icelandic volcano had its strop, and we were stuck there for a fortnight. 'Be careful what you wish for' goes the old saw, and if you'd have asked me beforehand, I would have pretty much been up for two weeks in the blazing sun by a swimming pool in Israel with my best friend. So unpleasant was the experience, however, that I found myself kissing the ground at Gatwick and vowing never to return. Which I nevertheless did within the year – women, eh?

When I told my Israeli friends that I planned to go to Eilat for a week, they all seem utterly perplexed. A couple of them laughed, thinking I was making some sort of lame joke – like 'I'm going to Blackpool for a week, and not during the political party conferences either – how adorably naff am I!' A surprising number of them hadn't been there since they were children, or even not at all. How could that be, I wondered huffily, when Israel was such a small country? Then I remembered embarrassingly that I'd only bothered to go once in my life to Scotland, a place of extreme beauty and culture, and that only for the Edinburgh Festival to go see a play about myself.

In Tel Aviv and Jerusalem, history is so in your face that however much you drink, you still feel compelled to go out and experience the present. It's like history has come up to you at a bus stop and pushed you in the chest, jeering rudely: 'You think you're tough, eh? Think you're clever? Think you're the Big I Am? Mate, YOU DON'T KNOW NOTHING!' And so you follow your tormentor, determined to learn from him. In Eilat, you could be anywhere. And there are lots of children. And the hotels are a bit rubbish, though really expensive. (Jews aren't naturally good in the service industries, quite understandably, and because the trades unions are strong there – unlike the surrounding Arab states, where it's so cheap to holiday simply because the places were built by and run on non-unionized slave labour – it's extremely pricey, even to a sailor-on-shore-leave big-spender like me.) And no one drinks as much as you and they look at you like you're weird for wanting to start at 11 AM – but the way you see it, if you apply Hawaiian Tropic Factor 5, featuring mango, papaya, guava, avocado and passion fruit, first thing in the morning, and then have a Cosmopolitan and a bottle of Yarden wine along with your breakfast at Café Café, you've already had your five-a-day fruits. And your hangover sticks with you with all the dogged perseverance of a swotty exchange student intent on learning the lingo from you and you alone, and before you know it...you're hating the people around you. Who just happen to be Jews.

In Eilat, Nadia and I lurched from disaster to disaster, breaking heels and losing our dignity all the way. It started badly; my poor friend, who was so philo-Semitic she made me look like Abu Hamza (and so quick-tempered she made me look like the Dalai Lama) had the 'Why are you called Nadia?' line put to her by Israeli officials so often that she threatened to wear a sign around her neck saying in large letters: HELLO, MY NAME IS NADIA. MY MOTHER WAS ITALIAN AND MY FATHER WAS A SERB AND IN BOTH THESE NATIONS IT'S A VERY COMMON NAME. THE ARABS STOLE IT. Though I generally love the feeling of hassled solidarity with Israel I experience when queueing up for security at the El Al check-in; when they get to the part where the young man or woman says 'There is a reason I am asking you these questions', tears always spring to my eyes and I REALLY have to stop myself from blurting out 'I UNDERSTAND – I UNDERSTAND IT ALL! MY LIFE FOR YOU, ISRAEL!' in case they think I'm a loony and stop me from boarding.

You don't go to Israel and expect a servile minuet of bum-sucking etiquette from the hospitality industry – or even decent service. There are exceptions, of course – my advice is always to look for the big DAN Hotel sign when you visit a new Israeli city and walk straight towards it. In Eilat, separated from my beloved husband of the same name when the volcano went off and no one could say when it would be safe to fly again, this also became a source of sorrow, and just a glimpse of the big DAN sign in the night sky could start me wailing. Once in Tel Aviv, I looked up at the beautiful Sea One building, still under construction, and told Nadia, 'That's where I'm going to live.' But of course she'd been hearing it for seven years: she pointed back at the DAN sign flickering in the distance – 'No, THAT'S where you live...'

The shoddiness of our hotel experience in Eilat was hard to fathom, unless it was actually an elaborate joke. Sweltering in the Negev desert, on the border with Egypt, Eilat's sun-baked vista is a long way from Royston Vasey, the grotesque village of in-breds and xenophobes featured in the television show *The League Of Gentlemen*. It's a lovely place, no doubt about it, as chavtastic as the Promised Land gets – Jewish chavs, what's not to like! With a flourish typical of this cheeky city, it was the final piece of land reclaimed in the Israeli War of Liberation of 1948–49, and having forgotten to bring a national flag with them, the Negev Brigade soldiers improvised with pen and bedsheet and raised the glorious 'Link Flag.' It is a city which lives mostly horizontal, often stoned, with arms wide open, but even the devout are not immune to its louche charms. One of my best memories of the place, as I took a leisurely Israeli breakfast at Café Café – scrambled eggs, peppers, olives, tuna, feta and aubergine in a plate like a painter's palette – on the Eilat prom was watching the wholesome frolics of the pair of young Orthodox men in full garb who stood, fully clothed, in the sea, entreating their modestly-dressed, uproariously-laughing wives to join them. When they did, to a splashy cavalcade of connubial bliss, I couldn't help contrasting the sheer Jewish relish of life which lives so easily alongside the most fervent faith to what seems to me to be the grim and hypocritical joylessness of Islamism.

The frum certainly had fun that day, but sadly my experiences with Eilat hotels very much reminded me of the saying 'A Local Shop For Local People', wherein the proprietors see potential customers as pests and far prefer to run their business for their own satisfaction. One of them was situated on a part of the 'North Beach' which was not a beach at all but a barren mudscape, scattered with vicious sea urchins – probably working for the Egyptians, as a counter-attack on those sharks, birds, rodents and insects who have been accused of being Zionist spies by Arab states. On our first morning there, we went down to breakfast and sat in the empty half of the restaurant; only after scarfing down a good section of the breakfast buffet did we come to understand, by the various tutting faces and shoo-ing gestures of the staff, that we had inadvertently outraged the kosher food rules. As we trooped back to the other half of the hotel restaurant, our embarrassment among these people we admire above all others pathetic to behold, I bleated 'But we only had vegetables!' However, onlookers continued to give us angry stares, which seemed to imply that we had been caught redhanded attempting to force down the throat of a Jewish toddler a dirty great bacon sandwich, washed down with a chocolate milkshake.

The next day, unbeknownst to us, was Yom Hashoah, commemorating victims of the Holocaust. Not knowing this, when the siren started up, we were prone on our loungers with our eyes closed, laughing away as usual when Nadia suddenly said, horrified, as she opened her eyes to reach for a cigarette: 'Julie, everyone's standing up with their heads bowed. Even children.' We scrambled to our feet just as everyone sat down and resumed talking – probably about us and what a pair of disrespectful skanks we were.

This hotel had a swimming pool of the type of which I am particularly fond – cold, rectangular and unadorned by water slides; the classic lap pool. Before 10 AM, it was heavenly. And from 10 AM until sundown, it was a cross between *It's A Knockout* and Bedlam, as the biggest collection of anarchic brats – from ages 5 to 15 – you've ever come across outside of a Hampstead crèche used it as a makeshift playpen, urinal and wrestling ring. Occasionally, just to add to its tranquil allure, older teenagers chased each other around it wielding cans of shaving foam – invaluable in any idyllic setting, I find, when one gets the impulse to perform the classic A over T pratfall, as in one's favourite bits of *You've Been Framed* – which they sprayed with the same enthusiasm and generosity with which Evian mist is in more sedate establishments. The sheer volume of tossed footballs in alleged sun-lounger areas came to remind us quickly of Double Netball on a particularly hormone-heavy afternoon.

Attempting to chill out at a hotel spa is always another fool's errand in Israel, in my experience. No matter how many tonnes of combined single pebbles they place on reception desks, it struck me that this most fit, active and impatient of peoples are the most difficult of all to imagine wallowing in mud – unless it was to clear out a swamp in order to plant an olive grove. Always mindful of over-idealizing the Promised Land and its people, I asked my Hebrew teacher Yael Breuer, an Israeli living in Brighton, for her opinion. She said:

'A few years back when my family wanted to spend some time in the lovely Galilee and Golan areas and were looking for a place to stay, I was amused (and a little irritated) to find that in practically all descriptions on the websites of the quite simple B&Bs I was looking at, the word "mefanek" was used. Mefanek means pampering, spoiling, treats and every single website boasted of their mefanek ambience – luxurious, relaxing and healthy with, of course, no end of holistic treats. It is clearly a popular niche – and one which the average restless Israeli might actually benefit from – but there is something quite comical about it. There was a very funny sketch on Israeli television once about a group of friends who go on a spa break and nearly have a nervous breakdown when they realize that their relaxing, mefanek weekend does not include a TV in the room, the food is vegetarian – and that quiet, peaceful conduct is expected from the guests...'

We stayed at another Eilat hotel on a proper beach, probably the priciest one in town; if Liberace and Cecil B. De Mille had designed a love-nest together, it would have looked a lot like this. Leering life-size jester statues are frozen forever in mid-caper, and prancing golden ibex and horned rams preen by the swimming pool where stone cats spit spume upon the hapless splasher. The art on the walls was beyond kitsch – simple shepherds ceasing their desert travails to stare in dazed wonder at this shimmering citadel we now stood in. Or maybe, like us, they were merely hallucinating from dehydration, as this fancy-pants palace appeared to have just one staff member to every hundred guests, so slow was the service.

Limping back to Tel Aviv and the arms of the Dan, I could see why certain of my Israeli friends saw Eilat as only slightly more likely a holiday destination than Iran. We dropped our bags and headed straight out to Mike's Place, the best blues joint beyond New Orleans and just a Woo Woo's throw from the ocean, for quesadillas and Key Lime Pie shots, the door signs GOOD PEOPLE GOOD FOOD AND GREAT BEER and ENGLAND FANS WELCOME reflecting the easy-going welcome extended to all. This is despite the fact that on 30 April, 2003, a suicide bomber approached Mike's Place and blew himself up at the entrance, killing three people and wounding more than fifty. One of the wounded was a security guard named Avi Tabib, who blocked the bombers, preventing them from entering the bar and causing further destruction.

The attack was carried out by two British Muslims in their twenties, one of whom fled the scene after his bomb failed to detonate, with all the dignity and grace we have come to expect from Islamist hysterics. His body was identified a month later after being washed ashore on the Tel Aviv beachfront. Mike's Place re-opened on Yom Ha'atzmaut, Israeli Independence Day.

On the way back to our hotel we stopped to look at the metal sculptures of a ship and waves which I'd never really noticed before, so neatly do they fit into the walkway leading from the Dan to the sea. They are part of the Aliya Bet Memorial Gardens, a beautiful tribute to the second wave of homecoming diaspora Jews mythologized in one of my favourite films, *Exodus*. I couldn't help reflecting that back then the British government terrorized Jews, and now British terrorists do. For a split second it made me feel ashamed – and then it made me proud, to have chosen my side so unconditionally.

I love Israel and I love the Israelis – even when they're rude, crude, impatient, ungrateful and brusque, which sounds a bit like a dissing version of that poem which goes 'How do I love thee? Let me count the ways...' I've got quite a few friends, otherwise sensible people, who come back from Israel bristling indignantly about the 'arrogance' of its people. But I think the problem is that most other countries make a great show of 'hospitality' while secretly despising tourists whereas Israelis treat tourists the way they treat each other – they are simply very honest, and compared to Arab 'hospitality' in particular, it can look rude. But give me the Israeli habit of leaving out a few please and thank you's any day over the surrounding countries' violent veering between the sucking up to and the cutting down of the Infidel.

I realized that I needed to check my reality when I found myself getting irritated at a group of cute, noisy Israeli tots playing Hide and Seek around some hotel terrace seating where Nadia and I were setting about the serious business of getting slaughtered at noon. Within living memory, Jewish children were hiding in fear of their lives. If they were found, they'd be killed – more than one million of the six million were children. But thanks to this impossible country, it now actually WAS a game. They were hiding for fun, not fear. They weren't there for my convenience – I was there for theirs, to pump a bit of extra cash into the tourist economy. I thought of an exchange my friend Chas had had with a friend:

Friend of Chas: 'I just find that when I smile at Jews in the street, they don't always smile back at me.'

Chas: 'Aww, naughty Jews, not lap dancing for you. And after all they've gone through, you'd think they could at least spare us a smile, eh?'

The first time I went to Israel, my present husband cried and my ex-mother-in-law (a Jewish atheist) informed me solemnly that she would pray each day for my safe return. When I went last, returning with a gorgeous suntan the week before Christmas, my response to enquiries about where my pulchritudinous pigmentation had come from evoked such reactions as 'Wow, you are brave!' Yes, it certainly took a lot of guts to eat pizza in Jerusalem, drink cocktails in Tel Aviv and lie on a beach in Eilat. I should get a medal, for my bravery.

SEVEN

THEY'RE BACK!

When I was a redneck teenager still in the calf-country of my philo-Semitism, so little contact did I have with Jewish culture that, risibly, one of my most prized possessions was a slender paperback called *BEST JEWISH JOKES*, which I guarded with all the fervour of a young talmidah protecting the Holy Book from the Philistines. (Or indeed, my Velvet Underground records from my mother.) Though it's been almost forty years, I can remember some of the gags to this day:

1. Mrs Cohen is in bed with her lover when Mr Cohen walks in. Mrs Cohen: 'Oh no, there's Blabbermouth – now EVERYONE will know!'

2. Mrs Cohen tells Mrs Steinberg. 'Don't tell anyone, but I'm having an affair!' Mrs Steinberg; 'Oy vey – who is doing the catering?'

3. Mr Cohen is in financial hot water. He confides in his wife who produces a vast jar of silver coins. He embraces her and cries, 'We're saved! Where did all this money come from?' Mrs Cohen blushingly admits, 'Well, every time you made love to me during our thirty years so far of marriage, I put a shilling in the jar...' 'Oy!' cries Mr Cohen, striking his forehead, 'why didn't you tell me? – I would have given you all my business!'

Two things strike me about my memories of this book. One, what a very busy lady Mrs Cohen was. And two, how very gentle even a book which might be broadly described as 'racist' was back then – a genteel world full of gents and ladies, Sams and Sadies, who always wore hats in the street and cried when their grandchildren passed exams.

When I walked around trying out these jokes on my fellow Gentile adolescents who, like me, had never met a Jew but who, unlike me, were uninterested in humour which did not involve base bodily functions and preferably end with a dead leg, I was met only with bafflement. These days, no doubt, those same kids might possibly say 'Yeah, effing Jews – picking on the poor Palestinians like that. Hitler was right!' For in the brutal, modern anti-Semitic humour which usually masquerades as anti-Zionism (Nazism writes the pamphlets. Islamism graffitis the synagogues) the old-fashioned envy-turned-hatred that the ugliest and stupidest Gentile has for the sexy and clever Jew has been souped up with a topcoat of caring about the alleged underdog – the Palestinians.

Interestingly (and paradoxically, to anyone with more than two brain cells to rub together) the all-importance of being seen to be anti-racist when it comes to colour has freed comedic cretins up to be as anti-Semitic (Jews are white!) as they please. There's an interesting parallel to this in a recent survey which showed that green consumers are more likely to lie and cheat than non-organic buyers; it's called 'moral licensing', apparently. But you might know it better by its previous name: hypocrisy.

And nowhere is it more prevalent than in contemporary comedy, where men who would never dream of using the n-word nevertheless fling about the c-word with pathological, gynophobic frequency. For a while, we were told that it was just a word like any other. Then came the rape jokes and the rape T-shirts, all in the name of 'banter.' It's like all the hatred which comedians used to direct at people of colour they now direct at women – and Jews. Progress!

The cowardly, preening, calculated bullying practised by comics as different as Jimmy Carr and Frankie Boyle seems to be based on the rule, 'Don't pick on anyone who might hit you'. That's why the jokers steer clear of straightforward race jokes, while bashing women, the handicapped and the Jews. 'There's nothing as sad as the laughter of those who have lost their faith,' someone once said, and I believe that something happened awhile back which literally left people not knowing whether to laugh or cry, and while it may have made them free, it certainly didn't make them happy. I think rap music had a hand in it; n-word this, ho that, bitch the other. When white middle-class liberal men started quoting, gloating and getting off on the gynophobic geometry of rap, that's when this climate of abuse started. It was being stopped, and then it was resurrected – just because there was now a culturally legit way for men to call women names. This kind of right-on sexism came to a grisly climax when Malcolm Black-man, the leader of the Anonymous UK protest group, was found not guilty in 2013 of raping a female fellow anarchist – but did admit to keeping a 'tally' of his sexual conquests on the outside of his tent, as a 'lads joke' and to 'boost morale' in the protest camp outside St Paul's Cathedral.

And what rap did 'for' women, us lucky ladies, the anti-Zionist movement has done for Jews.

How I remember with affection the large I HATE STU-DENTS badge I wore through my punk years! For I have no doubt that it is a vile minority of students who have driven and are driving the current climate of abuse against both women and Jews through the medium of 'humour'. Now that privileged white Gentile men can no longer be assured of stepping straight from 'uni' into a dream job, what a relief it must be to blame uppity women and Jews for one's less than sparkly prospects, rather than one's own mediocrity. Add to this fact that the Comic Commu-nity appears to contain an exceptionally high percentage of poisonous people, and that stand-up is the bog-stan-dard student's Big Night Out of choice, and you have the spot-on blend of bitterness and bile which can be easily whipped up into a perfect storm of nastiness which sees both female and Jewish students under attack on univer-sity campuses as never before in this country.

The myth of the Tragic Clown is a popular one, but it is always assumed that the Clown is Tragic because he is something of a pure soul who feels things deeper than most of us. But the way I see it, most of the misery the tragic clowns feel is down to the fact that they are really unpleasant people – intelligent enough to know this, but not intelligent enough to change it. At the end of Trevor Griffiths' 1975 play *Comedians*, the apparent hero, the veteran music hall comic who until this moment seems to be the moral compass of the piece, reveals that he became sexually excited when visiting Auschwitz after the war. In this vein, we can understand the apparently lunatic ability of the apparently Jewish writer Simon Louvish to write fondly of Spike Milligan in the *Guardian* (of all places!) in 2003: 'Spike's lack of boundaries led him inevitably to fall foul of society's current prohibition on racial stereotypes, which were part and parcel of his upbringing and age. He could no more avoid insulting Jews and "wogs" than he could avoid breathing.' This is probably a reference to the repellent Milligan's creation 'Mrs Rita Goldberg of Golders Green, playing a cash register while wearing a large plastic nose.'

Similarly, jokers who would never dare cross Muslims (who are, in my opinion, far inherently funnier than Jews; the 72 virgins who wait for random killers of innocent civilians outdo any other religion for sheer mirth value) feel free to bully Jews.

In 2006, Jamie Glassman wrote in the *Times* of his visit to that year's Edinburgh Festival during which he claimed that members of an audience yelled 'Throw them in the ovens!' during a routine by an Australian comedian, Steve Hughes, about Jews and Nazis. When this was put to him, Hughes performed an amazing act of self-aggrandisement with no apparent irony when he said that Glassman's piece had appeared during Israel's 'botched invasion' of Lebanon: 'Who owns *The Times*? Rupert Murdoch. [Glassman and Murdoch] were definitely searching for anything to take the onus off Israel doing anything bad.' An unknown Australian comedian picking on Jews in a basement in Scotland – guaranteed to take the eyes of the world off conflicts in the Middle East every time. Such easy linking of the plight of Jews, the actions of Israel and the Zionist control of the media does nothing to make us give Hughes the benefit of the doubt in this situation.

When I was growing up, it seemed like there was a statute of limitations on Jew-hatred – but now it's been open season for some time, as jokes about other races have become unacceptable. And there are no moral barriers whatsoever – don't expect Jewish children to get off scot-free. (They never do – one million of the six million Jews murdered by the Nazis were children, after all.) There was no State of Israel when Anne Frank was hunted down and murdered, but this didn't stop the repellent Chris Evans from finding her persecution amusing in 1996 on Radio One, or the hideous David Mitchell from doing the same in 2009 on Radio Four. And as for Frankie Boyle, who went from picking on handicapped children to picking on Jews, could he not just bully a handicapped Jewish child next time, thus streamlining his act? The big, brave hero!

*

Campus anti-Semitism starts with the toe of humour dipped in the water of public tolerance – and ends up with Jewish student associations hounded into hiding, in fear of their own safety.

In 2008, at Oxford University, students held something called a 'Bring A Fit Jew' party – at a curry house! – at which they were told to arrive dressed as Orthodox Jews, complete with sidelocks, carrying bags of money. One of the organizers – a creature with the unlikely name of Phil Boon – when told how 'isolated and vulnerable' such acts made Jewish students feel, said he 'didn't see what the problem was...I can understand why it might have offended some people, but it would have been an awesome social...all the Jewish girls who had been invited were really looking forward to it.' Another student involved said he thought the theme was 'fairly good banter.' Banter again! Can't you just imagine the EDL and the BNP shrugging incredulously, innocent-eyed, when THEIR banter is misapprehended by a load of humourless Jews and blacks? Banter truly has become the fetidly-filled nappy with which cretinous cowards cover their collective arses.

But anti-Semitism, be it banter or in deadly earnest, has been around at institutes which ironically seek to educate for a long time. The writer Laura Marcus told me

Campus anti-Semitism was rife when I was at college in the late 70s. The worst offenders by quite some way were the far left, particularly the SWP. They'd use anti-Zionism as an excuse but it was anti-Semitism. Our Jewish Society had to fight to keep its NUS funding which all clubs and societies got because our SU, same as most at that time, had a 'no platform for racists' policy. And some tried to say that WE were racist because we supported Israel. I'd come up against anti-Semitism at my totally WASP secondary modern where I was the only Jew in a school of 900! But this was different. This was disguised. This was, oh we're not anti-Jews or anti-Semites. We're just anti-Zionist. Always felt anti-Jewish to me.

When I edited the student newspaper in my final year one of the members of the pro-Palestinian group came in, with a couple of his friends, to tell me to put a two-page centre pull out in the newspaper promoting their cause. I refused. Said I would refuse to do that for anyone. You couldn't just commandeer two pages of a 16-page newspaper. He got very shirty with me but I stood my ground. Naturally I was accused of being anti-Palestinian but way I saw it, I was being pro-journalism. It wasn't the few Arabs and Palestinians at the college that bothered me though. It was the middle-class, well-heeled, left-wingers who were just camp followers desperate for a cause.

Anyway that aside, it was a happy time at college. But I do recall feeling a bit lonely because I couldn't really share all this with anyone. My boyfriend at the time and all my friends were non-Jews. Hey ho, the wandering Jew. Never feel you belong anywhere.

Fast forward to 2013 and the wandering of the Jews

around the nation's campuses becomes a frenzied pinball ricochet as they are pursued from pillar to post to safe house in a grotesque miniaturization of all the night-time flights that came before. Reading the information page of the Jewish Society at St Andrew's University, it's hard not to be touched by the sheer mild-manneredness of it – less manifesto than polite request not to be punched in the face repeatedly, please! – with its bagel lunches, beach barbecues, Friday night dinners. The sorrow, as with so much of the Jewish story, is in the sparseness – there is no kosher accommodation in the town, kosher food has to be ordered in all the way from Manchester, the nearest synagogue is in Dundee 'although services there are not regular given the very small community' and 'there is one Jewish family in St Andrews, so the society is really the only community.'

Given this, it makes it all the more remarkable – even by the positively subterranean moral standards of Western Palestine-panderers – that when these isolated and polite people sought to hold a dance at St Andrews Golf Hotel, it had to be cancelled after the establishment received threats from protestors objecting to the planned proceeds from the shindig going to support charities including the Jewish National Fund, the Friends of the Israeli Defence Forces and ELEM, a homeless charity bringing aid to both Jewish and Arab youth in Israel. A spokesman from the Glasgow Jewish Representative Council expressed surprise that the hotel 'had caved in so easily to intimidation'. Having seen how golfers dress, I find it hard to believe that a habituation of men en masse wearing go-to-hell trousers could be easily intimidated. And how poignant that, historically, golf once had such a reputation for anti-Semitism in this country, and was now complicit in making Jews feel less than human once again.

What makes traditionally right-on students think that it is perfectly OK to pick on an ethnic group like this? Some of it must be because that, as I've said before, modern anti-Semitism is generally different to other sorts of racism in that it includes a larger component of envy to that of contempt, due to the phenomenal success of the Jews despite all the barriers put up to block them. Indeed, what makes the current harassment of Jewish students seem especially savage and cruel is the fact that Jews have only been allowed to pass unhindered into university education for a relatively short time; in Oxford, for example, it was only in 1856 that Jewish students were accepted. In Anthony Julius' brilliant study of anti-Semitism in England, *Trials Of The Diaspora*, he quotes from private notes made by officials of the Cambridge University Appointments Board about two Jewish undergraduates which somehow became public:

Not very appetizing looking – short and Jewy with wet palms...I fear an unattractive chap – if only because one is instinctively drawn to feel this about the chosen race from which he must surely stem.

Of course, the physical appeal of English male academics of a certain age is so stare-into-the-sun dazzling that it is in some way at least slightly understandable that they are less than tolerant of the shoddy appearances of the rest of we mere mortals. On the other hand, this does seem to be something of a high-falutin' version of the familiar one-handed cyber-troll refrain 'Whoah! Wouldn't touch it wiv yours, M8!' – which invariably comes from haggard masturbators busily engaged in the pressing business of attempting to find their arse with both hands before inserting something in it.

Maybe part of the reason for some students when it comes to picking on Jews stems from envy. Maybe, also, in some cases, after years of being the weediest and/or weirdest kid in your class, it feels good to be the bully, even if you pretend you're bullying someone in the course of standing up for someone else. But I can't help thinking that there is an element of manqué see, manqué do involved.

In Iowa in 1968, the teacher Jane Elliott devised the blue-eyed/brown-eyed exercise to teach her class of eight-year-olds about the effects of racism. The blue-eyed children were given extra privileges while Elliott chastised the brown-eyed children – around whose necks the blue-eyed children had placed brown collars as a means of easy identification – if they refused to accept their inferior role. She noticed that the interaction and attitudes of the two groups to each other changed within the first fifteen minutes of the exercise. To quote Elliott's Wikipedia entry:

Those who were deemed 'superior' became arrogant, bossy and otherwise unpleasant to their 'inferior' classmates. Their grades also improved, doing mathematical and reading tasks that seemed outside their ability before. The 'inferior' classmates also transformed – into timid and subservient children, includ-

ing those who had previously been dominant in the
class. These children's academic performance suf-
fered, even with tasks that had been simple before.

Little did Jane Elliott know that, in the case of academics
and the Jews, this would become a sort of How To rather
than a Please Don't in many British institutions of further
education in the 21st century. For the inter-student
harassment has been a mere echo of the poisonous anti-
Jewish activity taking places among the teachers of those
students.

Those who support the academic boycott of Israel see
their activities as similar to those against South Africa in
order to pressure the government to end the apartheid system; those of us against it see it as being somewhat like
the Nazi boycotting of Jewish businesses in the 1930s. It's
pretty fair to say that the two sides aren't planning to join
up, hold hands and sing 'I'd Like To Buy The World A
Coke' anytime soon; both sides simply cannot give an inch
on the issue as they see the other side as so misguided. I
won't even pretend to be objective here – heck, if the IDF
were to burst in now and shoot me through the head I'd
probably try to find a rationale for their behaviour with my
final dying breath – but at least I'm well aware of my bias.
The other side, on the other hand, believe that they are the
still small voice of reason when in fact they are just the latest bigots to add their bellow of Jew-hatred to the one that
resounds down the centuries.

Like all wondrous, magical, life-enhancing things, the
idea of an academic boycott of Israel started with a letter
to the *Guardian*, in 2002. Before long it had 700 signa-

tories, who I'm sure were equally offended by the stoning to death of rape victims and the execution of gay men in the countries which surround Israel as by Israeli treatment of the Palestinians, but were washing their hair the night the letter suggesting a boycott of those countries also came around. It gathered strength later that year – though in the same way that a vandal will gather broken bits of paving stone rather than the way a young gazelle will gather vigour – when one Mona Baker, a signatory of the letter, working at the University of Manchester but originally from Egypt (whose nuts Israel so succinctly removed during their Six Day War of defence; six days on the lips, thirty five years on the hips!) in turn removed two Israeli academics from the editorial boards of two magazines no one's ever heard of which she and her husband publish. In an email to Professor Gideon Toury of Tel Aviv University, she said the following:

> *I will always regard and treat you both as friends, on a personal level, but I do not wish to continue an official association with any Israeli under the present circumstances.*

ANY Israeli! This is surely racism at its most brazenly unapologetic, made even sicker and sadder by the fact that Israel is not a country – unlike the Muslim slave-nations of varying complexions which surround it – where academics have to agree with the government in order to find work at government-funded universities. On the contrary, it is the academic community in Israel which holds the most liberal and pro-Palestinian views. Nevertheless, the bandwagon to boycott and isolate Israeli academics rolled on, picking up many a strange bedfellow along the way. In 2008 the University and College Union forwarded an anti-Israel link which came from the website of David Duke, the notorious white supremacist and Ku Klux Klan luminary – making the accusations that Israel practised apartheid seem approving rather than condemnatory.

The fetid fervency of the boycott bullies became even stranger when at its 2010 conference, UCU voted to support the boycott, divestment and sanctions campaign against Israel and, most eccentrically, to sever ties with the Histadrut, Israel's trades union alliance, declaring that it 'did not deserve the name of a trade union organization.' Compared to, one imagines, the organizations protecting the rights of the labourer in such worker's paradises as Dubai.

It is hard not to come to the conclusion that it is the sheer cleverness of Jews – a tradition carried on by the brilliance of Israeli invention and innovation, despite a good deal of superstitious surmising that the Chosen would only be clever when hounded from pillar to post to pogrom, for some weird reason – which has put the backs up among a great number of the worldwide academic community, and made them to keen to grasp any reason to harass them. If the man in the street can often become anti-Semitic because he fails to shine in comparison with this endlessly persecuted yet ceaselessly achieving group, how much more must the man on the campus get even more paranoid as he sees the Jews do effortlessly what he must burn the midnight oil to do, becoming a greasy grind in order to even keep within sight of them.

Even clever people fall prey to this fresh'n'funky, Just-Do-It brand of anti-Zionism. When Stephen Hawking became 'the poster boy of the academic boycott' in 2013, the irony was so immense as to render anyone with a sense of the ridiculous absolutely – well, speechless. The man who had used Israeli-invented science in order to be given an actual voice would now join forces with the rest of the silencers in order to take away the voice of Israeli academics.

Meanwhile in the bog-standard comprehensives of Britain, a world away from the Olympian heights habituated by Hawking, Jewish children and Jewish schoolteachers are persecuted with a casual savagery which makes one feel that the Nuremberg Trials never happened, by Jew-hating children and their staff-room sympathizers and apologists. In the *Jewish Chronicle* in 2012, a trainee teacher in an inner-London school detailed the surreal amount of aggression which she, as a Jew, had grown used to:

I dealt with countless remarks about my religion, ranging from the perplexing to the deeply offensive. After students drew swastikas all over the classroom, my supervisor said simply: 'It's not our job to project our own moral compass on to the students'... I found myself the constant prey of a group of roaming lower schoolers who would verbally abuse me everywhere and anywhere – including in my classroom – with screams of 'Hitler! Hitler!' Amazingly, each time I reported an incident, it was ignored. Knowing there would be no consequences, no discipline imposed on them, only encouraged the group. Later, someone scratched 'Kill Jews' on to a computer in my class-room. The school got rid of the evidence only after I involved the police. I could detect no racism towards the other, ethnically diverse staff members. Minor incidents of racist name-calling between students were always swiftly punished. Why were the endless attacks on me ignored?

Once more, surely the answer can only be that it is open season on the Jews. Who can blame one of my godchildren for bursting into tears when her Jewish identity was revealed to her as a teenager? 'I get picked on for being dyslexic and dyspraxic. And now I'm going to get picked on for being Jewish. Thanks, mum!'

What a world she has to look forward to! One in which anti-Semitism has become the default setting of every playground bully, from those who wear actual school uniforms to every famous freak from Mel Gibson to John Galliano to the veteran left-wing film-maker Ken Loach who said, in response to a report on the rise in anti-Semitism, 'If there has been a rise I am not surprised. In fact, it is perfectly understandable because Israel feeds feelings of anti-Semitism.' Lucky little girl, to become an adult in a world where anti-Semitism is not just surviving but thriving, BUT FASHIONABLE. With the hot new blood of Islam to give it strength, she can look forward to a lifetime of wishing she had never been told she was Jewish.

Indeed, and incredibly, she can expect to live in a

world which – in Britain at least – plays host to a new strand best described as Caring, Sharing Anti-Semitism, in which Jews are demonized and persecuted in an attempt by some wise souls to usher in a better world. Where I live, in Brighton, I spend many Saturday afternoons on a counter-picket outside an Israeli-owned recycling store, Ecostream. Rather than washing-up liquid and fizzy pop concentrate, you'd have thought they were selling fillet of panda and tusk of elephant the way the baying crowd bellowing for closure carry on. The height of hilarious hypocrisy came last year when a 25-year-old man – a social worker, yet! – gave our side a Nazi salute; by no means a uniquely elegant and well thought out expression of Palestinian solidarity, but easily up there with 'Blood-suckers!' and 'Fuck off, Jews!' which can be heard most weekends hissing across from them to us. A friend of mine had an even more hoist-by-their-own-petard moment; interviewing protesters outside a performance by an Israeli dance troupe, she asked one girl, 'People may say you're anti-Semitic. What do you say to that?' 'Yes. Yes, I am,' she smiled beatifically.

We have moved from a position where anti-Semitism was the hate that dare not speak its name – after the Nuremberg trials – to days where it is more than happy to scream it from the rooftops. A couple of years ago, Elie Wiesel, Nobel Laureate, said this:

Since 1945 I was not as afraid as I am now. I am afraid because anti-Semitism, which I had thought belonged to the past, has somehow survived. I was convinced in 1945 that anti-Semitism died with these

Jewish victims in Auschwitz and Treblinka. And now I see no, the Jews perished, but anti-Semitism in some parts of the world is flourishing.

Flourishing is a good word. In the sunshine of Third World fever, what once looked like a dying pleasure of sad old white men is suddenly alive with the rhythm of self-righteous right-on-ness, as the former Left sucks up to homophobic, sexist, racist Islamism on the principle that my enemy's enemy is my friend – even if he would stone me to death for adultery or execute me for being a filthy atheist. And to the east of Europe, in those charming countries now liberated from Soviet tyranny, the old freezing breath of anti-Semitism is enjoying a resurgence, as the newly independent states cling to the old certainties – that The Jews Did It being one of them. Regrettably, many – though not all – Eastern European immigrants have brought with them to Britain a racist attitude to Jews, blacks and Asians, which has further added to the pressure-cooker atmosphere of many inner-city multicultural schools. In 2012, Jewish organizations quite rightly became angry when a Ukrainian politician called the Ukrainian-Jewish actress Mila Kunis a 'zhydovka' – a 'dirty Jewess', a phrase not heard in that part of the world in the public sphere since the Holocaust, in which Ukraine played such an enthusiastic part.

Such a full-on pincer attack of 21st-century anti-Semitism is not the way to make Jews feel that Israel is superfluous to requirements, to put it mildly. And to those who say that Israel causes anti-Semitism, what was the cause of the anti-Semitism BEFORE 1948, when the modern state of Israel was established, including the Shoah? Then, Jews were murdered for being outsiders. As Amos Oz memorably wrote:

Out there, in the world, all the walls were covered with graffiti: 'Yids, go back to Palestine.' So we came back to Palestine, and now the world at large shouts at us: 'Yids, get out of Palestine'.

The fact that many Gentiles and Arabs are rabidly Judeophobic, while many others are as horrified by Judeophobia as by any other type of racism, makes me believe that anti-Semitism/Zionism is not a political position (otherwise the right and the left, the PLO and the KKK, would not be able to unite so uniquely in their hatred), but about how an individual feels about himself. Narcissism and (often quite reasonable) low self-esteem often come in one contradictory package, and those who tend to score high on this winning combo tend to resent the Jews.

A brilliant friend of mine, Phillip Mark McGough, put it better than I ever could:

Anti-Semitism appeals to the reptile brain, the irrational, magical part, which is why it's so seductive, accessible to all, a universal voodoo, and in a weird way brings a sort of negative unity – a unity of hostility – to an otherwise partisan world. All my adult life I've been a man of the Left: which is about boring stuff like equality, social justice, common sense, fair play – not reflex-action support for anything that says the right thing about Israel and America, no matter the cost in terms of ideological self-mutilation. The shotgun alliance between a certain strand of left-liberal thought and Islamism is one of the most emetic spectacles in modern politics. The Soviet Union at least preached a phoney egalitarianism. Islamism leaves them with no excuse. And with all the logic of a monkey sawing through the branch it's sitting on, no sooner is there another atrocity than the brooding introspection begins. 'What did we do to provoke this?' It's nothing to do with Israel, it's nothing to do with American foreign policy, it's to do with a barbaric credal wave reasserting an ancient title to the world. If Israel disappeared tomorrow, these people would still want to kill us. My only consolation – though it's a bitter one – is that it's the liberal left's own world-view which stands most at hazard here.

Even the Germans now feel safe enough in an Israel-hating world to be anti-Semitic again. At a Beyoncé concert in, of all places, Berlin in 2013, ten young Israelis arrived early and succeeded in seating themselves in the front row. Regardless of their long and ignoble history of annexing the sun-loungers of Mediterranean Europe, the Teutonic charmers took exception to this and began to harass the Israelis, yelling both 'Dirty Jews' and 'Go back to Israel.' At one point, some fifty people were yelling 'GO! GO! GO!' When the Israelis asked for assistance from a security guard, they were told 'You are ten and they are fifty.' Multiply that by millions, and it seems to me that we have been here somehow before, in some half-remembered sepia horror.

O shameful new world, that has such ancient creatures in it! In a final twist of bitter harvest, on the very same day – the 24th of May – as the Beyoncé-soundtracked hatefest took place in old Berlin, Germany was pronounced 'the most popular country in the world' in a poll by the BBC World Service.

Against the blaring cacophony of resurgent anti-Semitism – in stereo, yet, from cold-blooded Eastern Europe and the hot-headed Middle East – human intelligence is the only real weapon we have left. If it fails, then the new Dark Ages seem set to consume all of us who do not have the darkness inside of them to start with. It's like I said before – the Jews aren't known as the Chosen because they're up themselves, stupid, but because they were TOLD FIRST. They were told first, and the rest of us had a chance/the choice to listen, and we didn't. Now they are being told first again. If we turn away and choose not to listen, the cacophony of hate will one day blare in our ears too. But by then it will be too late to fight back.

EIGHT

THE NEW JEWS?

On 15 October, 2006, the *Sunday Times* ran an extraordinary piece of polemic by one India Knight, entitled 'Muslims Are The New Jews'. In my experience it's always best to reveal one's bitching back pages with adversaries using complete candour, so here's what happened immediately after I read it. ('Scuse fingers!):

To: letters@sunday-times.co.uk

From: Julie Burchill

Dear India Knight,

I dare you to walk into any mosque – after covering your filthy female head in the Islamist fashion, of course – and spread your glad tidings that 'Muslims are the new Jews.'

You'll be lucky if you get out alive.

Yours sincerely,

JB

PS: I see that your new book is a compilation of 'dirty bits' from novels. I'd love to know how this fits in with your new-found love of feminine modesty and discretion.

To: Julie Burchill

From: India Knight

Oh, for fuck's sake. I don't have a 'newfound love of modesty and discretion' – I just don't despise people on the basis of what they wear.

Regards,

IK

To: India Knight

From: Julie Burchill

What, not even the working class slags in crop tops you're forever slagging off, you hypocritical snob?

To: Julie Burchill

From: India Knight

I do NOT slag off working class people in crop tops, you fucking loon. Where? When? Why would I slag them off? I am many things but I am not a snob. God, you're driving me mad. Go away.

To: India Knight

From: Julie Burchill

I wrote to the letters page, not YOU, you stalking cretin. Why don't you fuck off and turn yet another of your husbands gay?

To be fair – as is my wont: see above – the piece in question started off reasonably enough. Knight expressed support for the suspension of Aishah Azmi, a teaching assistant working in Dewsbury, who refused to take off her veil in class. Azmi had been allowed to wear her mask everywhere else on school premises, but was asked to leave it off when actually doing her job; as the local education authority pointed out her pupils – most of whom were learning English as a second language – would benefit greatly from seeing her mouth move. And also, probably, because it wasn't Hallowe'en.

In Azmi's obduracy, we see a great metaphor for the contemporary Islamist – as opposed to the everyday ordinary Muslim, who just wants to rub along with the rest of us – experience in Britain; something akin to a man who voluntarily ties his legs together, and then rails at some outside power for forcing him to hop. I'll declare here my loathing for the walking shrouds which masquerade as symbols of religious pride – the niqab, abaya and burqa. Maybe I'm missing something, but I fail to see how one becomes closer to G-d by dressing like a parrot's cage that someone forgot to take the drape off of, never feeling the sunlight that the Lord created on one's face, and generally acting as though the body that the Creator gave one is some sort of dreadful mistake which is best served by literally drawing a veil over it. As the Somalian Muslim-born feminist apostate Ayaan Hirsi Ali said:

The veil deliberately marks women as private and restricted property, non-persons. The veil sets women apart from men and apart from the world; it restrains them, confines them, grooms them for docility. A mind can be cramped just as a body may be, and a Muslim veil blinkers both your vision and your destiny. It is the mark of a kind of apartheid, not the domination of a race but of a sex.

It's interesting, if we're going to compare Jews and Muslims, how the two groups deal with the ever-prevalent issue of lust. Pious Muslim men blame the woman and chuck a bin-bag over her; pious Jewish men blame themselves and take appropriate action. In the summer of 2012 I read about the craze for 'modesty glasses' among the ultra-Orthodox men of Mea Shearim in Jerusalem who wanted to stop eyeing up women – spectacles costing just a few quid, with a sticker on the lenses which makes it hard to look anywhere but straight ahead for a few metres. All else is a blissful, sexless blur.

Other 'modesty accessories' for men include blinkers, vision-impeding hoods and portable screens that can be used in airline seats to block passing women from view and prevent men from inadvertently watching in-flight films featuring scantily-clad starlets. Non-believers may sneer – but what a refreshing contrast to the Islamic habit of blaming the victim. Furthermore, Judaism teaches that BOTH sexes should dress modestly – whereas I cannot be the only infidel who has often been amused by the sight of a mismatching Muslim couple; she in full parrot-cage drag, he with trousers so tight you can tell his religion and slashed shirt revealing a medallion nestling in copious chest hair, for all the world as if he's on his way to a Gay Pride 'Come As Your Favourite Seventies Sex Symbol Crooner' fancy dress competition.

Knight went on to pillory the 'white, male' (such righteous, outsidery anger from an upper-middle-class female whose stepfather is a director of the newspaper group she writes for, and whose autobiography, if ever sprung upon a breathlessly waiting world, will probably not be called *My Struggle*) former foreign secretary Jack Straw for daring to voice his opinion that the veil is 'a visible statement of separation and of difference', and for being downright pervy enough to ask veiled women who came to consult him as their local MP to let him see their faces. Based on this evidence, Knight opined 'It's open season on Islam – Muslims are the new Jews.'

It's hard to know where to start when confronted with the stark, staring stupidity of this statement, Firstly, there's the hilarious, unconscious insult it imparts. Islam and Judaism have always been at loggerheads. Quite how Islam squares its hostility with the fact that three of its major prophets are Jewish is quite beyond me, but then Mohammedism – even compared to other belief systems, which by their nature may seem fanciful to the outsider – has never been strong on logic.

When in 2013 the Labour peer Lord Ahmed blamed the Jews for the fact that he had been sent to jail for the massive stretch of SIXTEEN WHOLE DAYS for killing a 28-year-old man, Martyn Gombar, with his Jaguar X-Type shortly after sending and receiving five text messages two minutes before the crash, lots of people were shocked. I wasn't. I just thought: 'They're back.' And then I thought: 'No – they never went away...' Useful idiots and fellow travellers – 'the silly led by the sinister' as Christopher Hitchens so memorably nailed the Not-In-My-Name marchers who called themselves anti-war but who actually wished Saddam Hussein to remain in office until dying a peaceful death in bed, surrounded by his family – like to pretend that Islamic anti-Semitism started with the re-invention of Israel in 1948, and that if Jewish European infidels hadn't suddenly set up camp in the middle of Arab Muslim land right out of the blue in the middle of the 20th century, then Muslims would be salaaming their Jewish brethren – who would be living peaceably amongst them, the beatific beneficiaries of that legendary Islamic toler-ance! – till the goats come home.

Sadly, Islamic anti-Semitism stretches all the way back to the inventor of Islam – when no lands were Muslim lands, and the Jews had inhabited their small, lovely coun-try since before the Bible. Why did it start? Was it envy that the Jews were the first monotheistic religion and Islam got there so late? This inferiority complex might explain the Islamic habit of wild over-compensation, such as insisting upon calling converts to Islam 'reverts' – as though we were all Muslims to begin with, which is obvi-ously not true looking at the start dates of the three Abra-hamic religions.

The prophet Mohammed allegedly initially admired the Jews for being the first switched-on monotheists, but grew angry with them when they resisted his calls to con-version to his brand new faith. (There's a reason why it's called monotheism; because there is only one deity, and the Jews found Him first.) Then there's the fighting thing. In theory, the Jews shouldn't be good at fighting – they're too brilliant at thinking. But right from the word go, the Jewish tribes of the Mecca area refused to submit to Mo's will, and were murdered in the field rather than become his new best mate. From thereon in, the bitching on the part of Islam against the Jews escalates. The words 'nag', 'repetition' and 'fiction' come invariably to mind when observing the number of sly digs against the Jewish people in the sacred texts of the Mohammedans. It must also be said that they seem irretrievably childish; there is a frankly astonishing number of references to evil Disney-style trees and stones who are willing to yell 'Hebe's behind me!' at the drop of a hadith. One of the verses is now part of the Hamas Charter; it reads

> But even if the links have become distant from each other, and even if the obstacles erected by those who revolve in the Zionist orbit, aiming at obstructing the road before the Jihad fighters, have rendered the pursuance of Jihad impossible; nevertheless, the Hamas has been looking forward to implement Allah's promise whatever time it might take. The prophet, prayer and peace be upon him, said: The time will not come until Muslims will fight the Jews (and kill them); until the Jews hide behind rocks and trees, which will cry: O Muslim! there is a Jew hiding behind me, come on and kill him! PS This will not apply to the Gharqad, which is a Jewish tree.

Sometimes the sheer lunacy of Islamist thought becomes so high on its own supply that Muslims themselves appear confused. The quotes about Jews hiding behind trees and rocks are not in the Koran – rather in the Hadith, the say-ings of the prophet Mohammed, so that's OK – but even the Egyptian government minister Talaat Mohamed Afifi Salem can say, quoting an alleged verse from the Koran, in 2013

> *We hope that the words of the Prophet Muhammad will be fulfilled: Judgment Day will not come before the Muslims fight the Jews, and the Jews will hide behind the rocks and the trees, but the rocks and the trees will say: Oh Muslim, oh servant of Allah, there is a Jew behind me, come and kill him – except for the gharqad tree, which is one of the trees of the Jews.*

That Jewish tree again! One almost sees its Fagin-like fronds reaching out to enfold its Israeli offspring in its decadent embrace. However, the Koran has its own problems:

> *(5:51) – 'O you who believe! Do not take the Jews and the Christians for friends; they are friends of each other; and whoever amongst you takes them for a friend, then surely he is one of them; surely Allah does not guide the unjust people.'*

Unjust people, pigs and apes...for all the talk about Islamic tolerance, the fate of the *dhimmi* under Islam has been dire, as described in Martin Gilbert's disturbing history of Jews in Muslim countries, *In Ishmael's House*. Though they were 'allowed' to perform their religious rituals, as were Christians, the display of non-Muslim religious symbols, such as crosses or stars, was prohibited on buildings

and the ringing of church bells or the trumpeting of sho-
fars was banned. Christians and Jews were also not
allowed to build or repair churches without Muslim con-
sent or to seek converts among Muslims. (On the part of
Christianity, that is; uniquely of the three Abrahamic religions, Judaism does not proselytize, as demonstrated in
the symbolic turning away of a prospective convert three
times.) Not being allowed to ride camels and horses, being
forced to wear one shoe or different coloured shoes,
attaching signs to houses and identifying marks to clothing
– the list of persecutions ranged from the petty and pointless to the frankly genocidal.

Another way in which Muslims differ wildly from Jews
is that while the rights of Christians are protected in the
Jewish state, they are currently going to Hell in a handcart
all over the Islamic world. To the present day, of course,
Christians and Jews are discriminated against in Islamic
countries whereas in Christian countries, and in Israel,
Muslims may worship in mosques, mostly as they please.
They may even fill these mosques with converts to Islam
from Christianity – whereas a Muslim who seeks to
become a Christian is committing the 'crime' of apostasy,
which is punishable by death in many Islamic states, thus
making sure that the conversion is all one way on a global
basis. This admirable regard for freedom of worship on the
part of the West can become a rather unhealthy cultural
masochism among Christian nations and church leaders,
such as when in 2008 the Archbishop of Canterbury
Rowan Williams said that certain aspects of the sharia
law might be adopted within British law in order to aid
social cohesion. Yes, because social cohesion really, really

flourishes when there is one law for one group of people and another law for a second. This pronouncement was made even stranger by Williams' declaration in 2011 that no Adam and Steve would ever become husband and husband in one of 'his' (rather than His) buildings, taking on the Islamic attitude to homosexuality in anticipation of the inevitable arrival of the sharia law which he seemed so intensely relaxed about three years ago, obviously.

It's at times like these I'm really pleased that I never bothered with that theology degree, if this is how confused you end up – lashing out at those who wish to be married by you, while embracing those who are murdering your brothers and sisters all across the world. So far as I know there is no country in the world where gay dictatorships burn down churches and execute those who chose to convert to Christianity. But there are many Muslim countries which do exactly this to Christians, who now make up the majority of those persecuted for their religious beliefs worldwide.

The writer Adrian Morgan told me:

There is something very dishonest about trying to prevent historical facts of Islamic anti-Semitism being discussed. We can easily discuss Christian anti-Semitism, massacres of Jews at Clifford Tower in York, the Jews who brought coronation gifts to Richard I being killed and robbed, followed by massacres of Jews of London, medieval blood libels, Nazism, Russian forgeries of the 'Protocols'. And no-one bats an eyelid. The biens-pensant agree with how horrible such cases were and nod sagely. But mention Islamic anti-Semitism in the same terms and quoting references and suddenly one is 'peddling hate', or is a 'fascist', a 'loon', and any attempts to discredit and smear the person who brings the message, forsaking all propriety and moral standards, can be brought to bear. Because this is a truth that dare not be spoken of publicly. Better to claim the messenger is a hater, or a liar. Why?

Search me, guv. But what is certain is that the first reactions of most Muslims on being told by Knight that they are any sort of Jew – new, old or sky blue pink – would be 'You COW! Outside – now!' Before, of course, the sneaky contingent among them stroked their beards and thought 'Hmm...hang on...'

But far worse than the unintentional – and rather amusing, considering her sucky-up intention in writing the piece – insult it pays to Islam (from Islam's own twisted point of view), Knight's statement deliberately insults Jews – their memory, their history and their suffering. In a particularly vile section of this piece, she recalls an unpleasant experience she once had while house-hunting with her husband:

My former husband and I once went to look at a house we were thinking of buying in a Jewish Orthodox bit of London. As it happened we were the only non-Orthodox people on that bit of pavement that morning. I noticed a group of Hassidim were walk-

ing around us in a peculiar way. 'They're avoiding our shadows,' the estate agent said. 'Because we're unclean.'

It's a lovely new side of India Knight we see here – not the sweary sexed-up sophisticate of her public persona, but rather A PERSON WHO BELIEVES WHAT ESTATE AGENTS SAY – bless! And quite a creative person, too – despite the evidence to the contrary supplied by her less than sparkling novels. A lawyer friend of mine, David Harounoff, told me:

This story is completely untrue and has no basis in any variation of Judaism. It's a hoax that has appeared in anti-Semitic productions of the Talmud and in anti-Semitic tracts in Eastern Europe. The India Knight 'estate agent' story is also a fabrication. I once challenged her to reveal the identity of the so-called estate agent or the address and she refused.

Interestingly, Knight's former 'partner' (otherwise known as a boyfriend who won't marry you) is the writer Andrew O'Hagan, who in 2006 in the *Daily Telegraph* offered his thoughts on Mel Gibson and anti-Semitism, after the actor indulged in a drunken outburst about Jews. He had previous, by the way – the actress Winona Ryder, née Horowitz, told a journalist that at a party in the 1990s, he had made a joke about the Holocaust to her. 'Somehow it came up that I was Jewish. He said something about "oven dodgers", but I didn't get it.'

Andrew O'Hagan certainly did, though, and apparently quite liked what he heard:

> *Dangerously worded as it was, Gibson's drunken comment was, it could reasonably be argued, a statement against the arrogance of the Israeli military: 'They started all the wars in the world.' Isn't it that which is making America call for his head? Of course it isn't even remotely true that Jews are behind most wars, but it is true that they are behind most movies, and pundits are saying that Gibson may never work again in Hollywood. But their response is overbearing and slightly hysterical.*

What a pair of open-hearted, clear-thinking charmers O'Hagan and Knight are! And what a shame they split; I would have paid good money to hear that pillow talk. But true or not (and it is rather odd to consider moving into an Orthodox Jewish neighbourhood and then complain about it being full of Orthodox Jews: rather like moving into Old Compton Street and then complaining that there are gays everywhere, or moving to Paris and complaining about French people) Knight's tale does provide a handy metaphor for the Jewish experience in Britain – particularly in the ways it is different from the impact that Islamic immigration has had on this country. And despite Knight's obvious preference for Muslims over Jews – somewhat crazily, she finds 'the Orthodox woman dressed in a drab sack and wearing a bad wig, as "weird" — weirder, actually — than a woman dressed in black with only her eyes showing' – there is a great deal that Muslims can learn from Jewish immigrants.

Walking around the shadows of the indigenous people is what the Jews have perfected to a fine art. Ducking, diving, surviving, thriving – and never once presuming that each new country they took up residence in owed them a living. Whether as trades unions activists or patrons of the arts – 'From Bethnal Green to Golders Green takes two generations', the old saying goes, though often they cut to the chase and do it in one: Lord Weidenfeld came here as a 19-year-old from Vienna with a postal order for sixteen shillings and sixpence – British Jews have always displayed great interest in their chosen home without ever losing sight of who they are. And SUCH self-starters! Consider the example of the Rothschilds; the first to arrive in England, in 1798, was Meyer, a penniless immigrant from a Frankfurt ghetto who spoke no English. His son, Lionel was elected an MP in 1847 but barred from taking his seat due to his religion. Only in 1858, after a change in the law to allow Jews to swear on the Old Testament (not the Torah) was he allowed to become the first practising Jewish MP, having won another election. His son Nathan was created a peer; his son Walter was a zoologist and the second Baron Rothschild. The current Lord Rothschild has four children – a boy and three girls – and while his son will inherit the title, no one yet knows how all the good stuff will be divvied up. It is a Jewish tradition that wealth is not passed though order of birth, but rather to the most able of the next generation, an example of cool-headed fair-mindedness which explains just a bit why the Diaspora Jews have traditionally out-performed every other immigrant group. Tellingly, in 2012, the daughter of the current Lord Rothschild said 'We shouldn't be in a series entitled *The Aristocrats*, because we're not. We're Jewish, which means we'll always be outsiders.'

There's an old joke about the sinking ship and the pastor, priest and rabbi. (This is the only clean version, so far as I know.) The pastor says 'My flock, there is no hope – just pray.' The priest says 'My flock, there is no hope, and anyway you deserve your fate because of your many sins.' The rabbi looks at his watch and says 'My flock, you have fifteen minutes to learn how to live underwater.' And there can be little doubt that Jewish success is greatly assisted by good sense and flexibility. Sadly, the Muslim experience often seems lacking in both – often on the part of those self-styled friends of Islam in the indigenous community more than many Muslims themselves, it must be said, who despite their avowed respect for said religionists often treat them with a lethal mixture of fear and condescension which brings to mind Kipling's 'half devil and half child' line from his poem *The White Man's Burden*. Awkward!

Look at inter-marriage. The Jewish rate of 'marrying out' is stratospheric, and looks set to get even higher. As far back as 1968, the then British Chief Rabbi and Head Worry Wart Dr. Immanuel Jacobovitz called for a meeting of Jewish leaders to deal with 'the critical problem of intermarriage' which he characterized as 'of catastrophic proportions'. It was then about 30 per cent. Another participant at the pious pity party, Rabbi Joseph Karasick of the Union of Orthodox Jewish Congregations, warned that if the rising rate of intermarriage were not reversed 'the whole fabric of the Jewish structure will suffer irreparable harm and damage.' Nevertheless, the trend has continued, as part of the progress of Planet Earth's general race-and-religion-mixing process which surely only the strangest sort of person could find fault with. Americans are now more likely to marry someone of a different faith than someone who supports a different political party and the Jews are as ever in the vanguard of enlightenment with a 1990 survey claiming that more than half of American Jews were marrying out. The latest statistic I could find for the UK was a respectable 44% – and this doesn't even take in the number of gay Jews who are now free to marry out.

In 1994 the new Chief Rabbi Jonathan Sacks published a book called *Will We Have Jewish Grandchildren?* which though serious in intent always makes me smile, the title somehow bringing to mind the old song 'How Much Is That Doggy In The Window?' But the question is far from a laughing matter for Dr Sacks, who warned:

> *The Jewish people, having survived for thousands of years in the most adverse circumstances, including the Holocaust, is today threatened by intermarriage and assimilation. Jewish communities throughout the diaspora are experiencing demographic decline. Why has this happened, and can anything be done to reverse the trend?*

But the way I look at it, why not spread the wealth? Going by that ever-shocking Nobel Prize strike-rate, Jewish blood may well create a more intelligent population, and it's surely a sign of strength rather than weakness that the

Jews don't feel a need any longer to cleave exclusively to their own kind anymore for comfort of all persuasions. It's quite natural to mock at in-breeding amongst humans – even though the historical cousin-marrying of the Ashkenazim, on the plus side, is thought to have given around 20 per cent of them a high resistance to HIV, cervical cancer and alcoholism. On the minus side, YOU'RE HAVING SEX WITH YOUR FAMILY! No wonder you go a bit crazy in the candy store when the opportunity presents itself.

Besides, many people who marry Jews choose to convert when faced with the sheer shimmering splendour of the original monotheistic religion. (There was a very amusing *Play for Today* on just this subject in 1977, *Oy Vay Maria*, in which the Catholic convert wife became a more enthusiastic Jew than her husband.) In a beautiful essay in the *Jewish Chronicle* in May 2013, Ben Rich explained why his Gentile wife – a shining example to our merry band of philo-Semitic favoured – made the leap of faith:

> *About 15 years ago, my wife leapt on to a Routemaster bus as it was moving away. She was followed by a woman in a hijab, who tripped. My wife grabbed her arm and pulled her on. And as the woman straightened up, she noticed my wife's Chai, which I had bought her on a visit to Jerusalem, and cried: 'Get your hands off me, you dirty Jew.' Rather than be upset, my wife – Rachael – responded by deciding that the time had come to convert to Judaism.*

He goes on to explain that two thirds of children of Jewish intermarriage identify as Jewish, even if their mother is a Gentile; an example of this is the splendid Paul Newman – Gentile mother, Jewish father – who once said that he nevertheless self-identified as a Jew 'because it's more of a challenge.' Rich concludes:

In fact, I never married out. My Judaism remained as strong as ever. Indeed, my relationship with my wife and the opportunity to re-engage with my identity through her eyes only enhanced my personal commitment.

We only 'marry out' if that's what we choose for ourselves, or how our community judges us. Every part of the mainstream community needs urgently to re-evaluate its attitude and approach to intermarriage and seize the opportunity arising from hundreds and thousands of wives and husbands who are only too willing to marry in.

Muslims, though, are a different story – 55 per cent of British Pakistanis are married to first cousins, and in Bradford, this rises to three-quarters – and it has produced a sad catalogue of birth defects and infant mortality. When the respected geneticist Professor Steve Jones drew attention to this regrettable state of affairs in 2011, the usual Muslim suspects got their knickers in a twist and proceeded to go through their tired old routine of shooting the messenger – or rather firing off a mindless press release aiming to discredit him. Mohammed Shafiq, chief executive of the Ramadhan Foundation, thundered, 'I find Steve Jones's comments unworthy of a professor. Using language like "inbreeding" to describe cousins marrying is completely inappropriate and further demonises Muslims.' (As opposed to marrying members of one's immediate family doing the demonizing.) Totally choosing to miss the point that Professor Jones had expressly pointed out that inbreeding was not confined to Muslims, and historically had occurred in every part of society, including the royal family: 'We are all more incestuous than we realise. There's a lot of surname diversity in London but if you look at the Outer Hebrides there are rather fewer surnames in relation to the number of people.' Before the imams rush to demonize geneticists, could they not try reading whole speeches by them, rather than just the bits alluding to them? And consider that the white working class of America – the charmingly-named 'white trash' – have been mocked as cousin-marriers for decades, and taken such joshing with unhissy good humour.

It won't do any favours for the Mohammedan gene pool – leaving aside that fact that the conversion of Lauren Booth might have brought the collective IQ down by a third – that, relative to other religions, an unusually high number of Muslim converts are convicts, or mentally ill, or ex-addicts and alcoholics seeking to maintain their old way of life with a spanking new righteous alibi; the girlfriend-beating criminal becomes the righteous jihadist without having to change his ways. The day after the soldier Lee Rigby was murdered by Islamist converts in London, another bright spark, Ashraf Islam – born Mark Townley – walked into a police station and helpfully told the police that he wanted to kidnap and murder Prince Harry. A jail-bird with a long history of fraud, he had seen the light in chokey and now the hunter had become the game as he fell for one of the biggest cons of all time.

With so many yobs finding Islamism appealing, little wonder that this 'religion of peace' has engendered a good deal of thuggish behaviour in this country in recent years – always under the guise of righteousness, natch. In 2011, many lucky residents of the London boroughs of Waltham Forest, Tower Hamlets and Newham woke up to find that a little helper had called in the night. But far from spreading joy and happiness, this night-caller was demanding doom and gloom, with posters instructing YOU ARE ENTER-ING A SHARIA-CONTROLLED ZONE – ISLAMIC RULES ENFORCED. NO GAMBLING, NO MUSIC OR CON-CERTS, NO DRUGS OR SMOKING, NO ALCOHOL. No fun, in short.

Hearing that no less than the tool's tool – and indeed the unofficial leader of Tools For Allah – Anjem Choudary had claimed responsibility for the attempted annexing of selected sections of the United Kingdom, and that he planned to cut a tool-shaped swathe through Muslim and non-Muslim communities alike in order to 'put the seeds down for an Islamic Emirate in the long term', one would be forgiven for thinking that the correct response would be hearty laughter, a slap on the Choudary back and a discreet email message to the dear creature showing him where he can find magic-men who promise to increase penis size. But this pantomime propaganda goes side by side with a far more sinister campaign of savage harass-ment of homosexuals and women in East London. For a couple of years now, stickers proclaiming certain London boroughs GAY-FREE ZONES have been appearing, while unveiled Asian women in the same unlucky boroughs have been threatened with violence and even death by Islamist thugs if they do not wear headscarves.

The proportion of Muslims in the borough of Tower Hamlets is around 36% – yet around 66% of the councillors are Muslim. This unhealthy state of affairs – where politics has more to do with tribal Bangladesh than modern Britain, and with cronyism more than comradeship – has been highlighted for some years in the Rotten Boroughs section of *Private Eye*. The grim roll-call of gangsterism on the part of the governing body of this Godforsaken fiefdom culminated in police reinforcements being called in to protect polling stations where Respect activists threatened other candidates with violence in 2012. The antics of these self-styled big boss men range from the ridiculous (the banning of biscuits in council meetings during Ramadan) to the rank (homophobic abuse yelled at gay councillors during council meetings going unpunished) to the revolting (numerous attacks on gay men by Muslim gangs.) Interestingly – India Knight, take note – the 'hood which is now fancifully called Tower Hamlets once played host to a large number of poor Jewish immigrants, and at no time did they attempt to gangsterize the place which they were lucky enough to call home. At no point did they attempt to impose their religion, culture and old-country ways on the indigenous population. They certainly never officially adopted 'Jewtown' as the official identity of their neighbourhood. In November of 2012, Mayor Lutfur Rahman – the colourful Mayor of Tower

Hamlets – united with Labour councillors against the local Conservative proposal to abolish the electoral ward of 'Banglatown', calling it a 'shameful attempt' to wipe out the contribution of the British-Bangladeshi community in the borough.

Originally a BNP slur, the adoption of Banglatown is telling, in that it accepts, even embraces ghettoisation and a lack of intent to become a fully functioning part of the country in which it exists. It explains why unemployment is so high amongst Muslim communities, why so many women are illiterate, why so many children do so badly at school. And it's NOT to do with the inherent racism of British society, clown, because Indian and Chinese children invariably do better than white British kids.

No doubt India Knight, bless her, thinks this sort of malevolent malarkey less 'weird' than walking round people's shadows, whether such a trek indeed took place in reality or in her imagination. But to anyone with a couple of brain cells to rub together, the Jewish example of how to join a nation is surely the more intelligent and enlightened one. Jews adapt themselves to the society they are in; increasingly, many Muslims seem to expect the society they voluntarily choose to move to (remembering that there are more than fifty Muslim countries in the world, many of them extremely wealthy and doctrinaire, which poor, devout Muslims might logically be expected to prefer) to adapt to them.

The meat of the matter – literally – can be seen in the different way British society has reacted to kosher and halal slaughtering practices. While kosher meat must be sought out, the lucky customer at Waitrose, Marks &

Spencer, Sainsbury's, Tesco, Somerfield, the Co-op, Domino's, Pizza Hut, KFC, Nando's and Subway can now pig out on ritually-slaughtered lamb and cow to his heart's content, as all these establishments put halal meat into their products without informing the consumer – a whopping 25 per cent of meat sales in Britain are now halal (hidey or otherwise) while only 3 per cent of the UK population are Muslims. And NO ONE'S that greedy – not even me.

It's not just flesh which seeks the Islamic seal of approval; such seemingly homespun products as Kelloggs, Kingsmill and Nature Crunch bars also 'adhere' to the Halal Food Standard. (Look for the cute little arched window on the packets.) Far from Muslims being the spat-upon pariahs that Knight would have us believe, we are – because of the greed and cowardice of corporations – having their belief system literally forced down our throats when we scarf an uncontroversial-looking bowl of cornflakes. It's this sort of mindless humdrum kowtowing to Mohammedism which adds to their lunatic idea that we were all 'originally' Muslims, hence the bugfuck-mental concept that people 'revert' rather than convert.

But even the Caliphization of carbs has not been enough for the likes of that careful driver Lord 'The Jews Did It' Ahmed, who worked himself into a right old froth in 2012 when told that he couldn't have halal meat in the Palace of Westminster as the method of killing animals – cutting their throats without stunning them – might offend non-Muslim colleagues. As it has been public knowledge since 2010 that many schools, hospitals and restaurants serve halal meat to unbelieving customers, you can sort of see his point; why should a bunch of unelected, stuck-up Lord and Lady Mucks get special treatment?

But on the other hand, people of Jewish birth have been in Parliament since 1802 – and I can find no record of them ever having asked for kosher food to be served in either house; again, that talent for adaptation. Which is not to say that all Jewish MPs are good guys. In 2012, a proposed bill to label all halal and kosher meat was blocked after Gerald Kaufman forced a vote. The Conservative MP Phillip Davies said, very reasonably, 'There are some people in this country who would wish to ban halal and kosher meat on animal welfare grounds. I am not one of those people – I'm happy for people to make the decision themselves – but they should be allowed to make an informed decision.'

Being in favour of informed decisions seems to me to be no-brainer, but not so to 'Sir' Gerald – who admittedly has had his own no-brainers in the past, so perhaps we shouldn't be too surprised at his sneakiness. This is a man, after all, who has compared the murder of his grandmother by Nazis to Israeli behaviour in Gaza; comparing Israel to Nazi Germany, a sure sign of a major loss to the Brains Trust. Kaufman has also compared Hamas members to the Jewish resistance during World War II, said of the gay-hanging, rape-victim-stoning Iranian government – while comparing it favourably to Israel – 'at least it keeps its totalitarian theocracy to within its own borders' and stated that the close proximity of affluent Israeli settlers to impoverished Palestinians is more 'heart-rendering' than conditions in South Africa during apartheid, as the bantustans were 'some distance away from the affluent areas'. So that's alright, then!

Islamophilia is a growing epidemic – long ago outstripping Islamophobia to become a disfiguring presence in modern public life – which blames all the crimes, misdemeanours and sheer screw-ups committed in the name of Islam on something else. As the writer Ben Marshall remarked to me:

> *Blame everything on the Jews and you cannot see, much less deal with your own problems. Refuse to educate 50% of your work force to their full ability, ban credit and promote the idea that there is only one book, the Koran, worth reading and then sit around scratching your head wondering why Muslim economies, even those with vast natural resources, consistently under-perform. Everything is always somebody else's fault – and I do mean everything. Economy? Jews, the West. War, America, the UK. Islamic terrorism? Nothing to do with Islam, and on and on it goes. It's like Islam has turned its adherents into one vast bunch of moody, recalcitrant teenagers. And then you have prize berks like Greenwald and Rusbridger coming on like* Viz's *'Modern Parents' – leave him alone, it's not his fault – he just needs more understanding...*

Right on cue, here is India Knight, from that 'New Jews' piece:

Especially since July 7, it has become acceptable to say the most ignorant, degrading things about Islam. And then we all sit around wondering why young Muslim men appear to be getting angrier and more politicised.

Isn't it funny how when groups of socially deprived young white men express bigoted, xenophobic sentiments, no one ever suggests that we should sit around holding their hands and telling them we feel their pain and understand where they're coming from? But let people a darker shade of pale do the same and we're all over them like a bad burka, positively encouraging them to scweam and scweam until they're sick, or indeed until they murder an innocent drummer boy on the streets of London? Well, it's better than BOTTLING IT UP, innit! How long will the ocean-going insanity of treating monomaniacal religious nutters as though they're nothing more harmful than a bunch of mixed-up but basically well-meaning Kevin the Teenagers continue? Even the government-funded unit set up to provide data and reports on attacks against Muslims is called Tell Mama. But if teenagers are ever to grow up, stop feeling sorry for themselves and get a life, endless pandering to their delusions of persecution are nothing but damaging – both to themselves and the society they live in.

A certain section of Muslims and their sheeplike supporters – the Grievance Ghouls – could really learn from the robust way in which British Jews have dealt with demonization, discrimination and persecution during their long and often tormented sojourn in this country.

Instead, they'd rather sit at home picking their sores, sneering at Christians and Jews as pigs and apes, believing that every out and proud gay man poses some sort of threat to their own unappetizing arses and dismissing free women as whores. The mentality which had one British Islamist, currently serving thirty years in jail, saying of the nightclub he and his moronic mates planned to blow up 'the biggest nightclub in Central London, no one can put their hands up and say they are innocent ... those slags dancing around' is the same mentality which led to the wholesale grooming (a deceptive word, calling up images of hair-brushing and toenail-paint, rather than full-on rape, torture, branding and DIY abortions) of white girl children as young as ten by Muslim men in the cities of 21st-century England. As Allison Pearson wrote in the *Daily Telegraph*:

Back in January, there was a profoundly disturbing case at Nottingham Crown Court. Adil Rashid, who had 'raped' an underage girl, was spared a prison term after the judge heard that the naïve 18-year-old attended an Islamic faith school where he was taught that women are worthless. Rashid told psychologists he had no idea that having sex with a willing 13-year-old was against the law; besides, his education had taught him to believe that 'women are no more worthy than a lollipop that has been dropped on the ground'. If Rashid had picked up that view in a madrassa in Karachi it would be pro-

foundly depressing, though not surprising. But the
school he attended was in Birmingham, voluntary-
aided – mainly funded by the taxpayer.

It is this mentality too, of course, which sees grown men shoot schoolgirls who seek an education through the head, and murder schoolgirls who, in their heartbreaking innocence, make films of themselves dancing fully-dressed in the rain. 'Honour killings' are in fact hate crimes of the most cowardly kind – and one which Jews seem agreeably disinclined to participate in. Yes, we all remember old Larry Olivier in *The Jazz Singer* rending his garments and kvetching away unconvincingly 'I HAFF NO SON!' when Neil Diamond had the nerve to marry Lucille Ball's shiksa daughter. But telling your children that they are dead to you – as only the most extreme Orthodox Jews do – when they marry out is a far cry indeed from actually murdering them for having fun and/or opinions, as quite a lot of Muslim men seem inclined to do.

It is a mentality which is, amazingly, aided and abetted by certain deranged women. We are used to the addled likes of Lauren Booth suffering from the side effects of extreme Stockholm Syndrome, but to read even non-Muslim women such as Knight advocating the Muslim way of life for women is extraordinary. Here she is equating dislike of the veil with being a slapper:

I am particularly irked by ancient old 'feminists'
wheeling out themselves and their 30-years-out-of-
date opinions to reiterate the old chestnut that Islam,
by its nature, oppresses women (unlike the Bible,

eh,?) and that the veil compounds the blanket oppression. In their view all Muslim women are crushed because they can't wear visible lipstick or flash their thongs. Does it occur to these idiots that not necessarily everyone swoons with admiration at the fact that they have won the freedom to dress like 55-year-old slappers?

And here's my highly unsisterly sister-in-law Charlotte Raven, who shamefully dismissed the plight of Afghan women under the Taliban thus in the *Guardian* in 2001:

Forced to construct a picture from the scraps of evidence gleaned from the media, I'd say the women spent their days crying and dreaming of lipstick while the men strode about barking theological maxims and beating their indomitable chests...there are times when the letter and law of the harshest definition of Islam can be reinterpreted according to personal preference. We don't know how often this happens.

With friends like these, who needs emetics?

Though the likes of Knight and Raven – Western, atheistic, privately-educated snoot-bags to a man – seem to believe that Islam has nothing to apologize for, it is telling that in June 2013 500 mosques around Britain were treated to a sermon entitled 'Tackling Street Grooming In The UK' during Friday night prayers, which highlighted

the responsibilities of Muslims to shun 'all forms of inde-
cent and immoral behaviour.' Better late than never:

> With so many individuals from a Muslim back-
> ground involved in such crimes, we have a responsi-
> bility to condemn this. We wholeheartedly condemn
> the disgraceful actions of those involved in these
> cases and welcome the convictions in the cases that
> have been through the courts.

And then they went and spoilt it all by saying something
stupid like:

> We need to tackle some of the root causes, which are
> quite often linked to criminality in some sections of
> our community and quite often connected to drugs.

This is, frankly, just a pious twist on the SHARIA ZONE
posters which warn off fun-seekers from certain postcodes
with a high Muslim population. The message here is that
criminals are to blame, not Muslims; that Islam, and its
inherent contempt for both women and non-Muslims,
might be part of the problem rather than most of the solution is never really considered. More religion, not less,
is taken for granted as the obvious cure for the disease.
Together Against Grooming spokesman Ansar Ali said the
campaign was born out a feeling of 'natural responsibility'
to condemn and tackle sexual grooming, explaining that
'The Koran and traditions of our Prophet exhort us to act
against evil and injustice, and create just societies. This is
the start of what will be a nationwide project in which we

seek to work with others to eradicate this practice from all communities. We are united in our stand against sexual grooming and, as Muslims, we are leading the effort to rid society of this crime.'

We all know a person who, after trespassing against us (often when intoxicated) steps up to the mark the next morning and apologizes. APPARENTLY. Because no sooner have we begun to react with delight at their noble shouldering of responsibility for previous unpleasantness than we realize that they are actually attempting to tar us too with the sooty brush of bad behaviour – in fact, to place that very incriminating item in our hapless hand. The idea that Muslims are leading the effort to rid society of the evil of abusing underage girls is as frankly ludicrous as the idea that the abuse of underage girls is a solely Muslim issue.

India Knight, whose essay inspired this chapter, seems to have no problem in generalizing about the Muslim mindset – 'My experience of Muslim life is not that it is the patriarchal nightmare of legend, but that women are powerful, vocal and iron-fisted beneath their velvet gloves' – so I'll have a bash too. And in summing up, I'd say that what the British Muslim community could learn, above all, from the experience of the Jews here is to be a bit less self-dramatizing. Don't run away with the notion that your lot are having the worst time that any minority group had in any country, ever. When Muslims commit atrocities – be they 9/11, 7/7 or Woolwich – try to appreciate the pain of the actual victims of those attacks rather than rush to bewail the backlash against you. You need to talk about Kevin the Jihadist, and make him realize the silliness of his universal strop, rather than blame the society which refuses to ceaselessly write him a sick note.

I am a life-long optimist, modernist and futurist – as I always say, if the past was so great, how come it's history? But as I get older, certain statistics make me feel 'Ooo, I'm glad I won't be alive much longer!' Sometimes the stats are about the state of the economy, and the nagging feeling I have that there will NEVER, EVER be a recovery – that it truly is closing time in the gardens of the West. But one of the numbers that makes me feel numb were the glad tidings, in May 2013, that one in ten Britons under 25 is a Muslim, that half of British Muslims are under 25 and that in 20 years there will be more Muslims than Christian churchgoers in Britain.

Who knows – India Knight could be right, and Muslims could well be the New Jews, who will bring a similar level of enrichment to this country. I, in turn, could be a vile bigot, and Islam's coming generations could turn out to be the most progressive and enlightened ever, embracing women's rights and gay pride and religious pluralism.

But what if they are not?

NINE

TOO COOL FOR SHUL

I've made a fool of myself quite a few times in my life – sometimes incidentally or accidentally, though more than once on purpose, just for kicks – but rarely as conclusively and publicly as when I attempted to convert to Judaism in 2009. Oy! Even now, writing this with no one but the cat in the room, I look around furtively to make sure no one's snickering at me. Because, truly, my efforts and their outcome were enough to make the cat laugh – even mine, Sox by name ('We'll spell it with an X to make him feel special,' suggested the life-affirming vet's receptionist the first time I took him for his shots), a serious soul who finds nothing in the least amusing.

Like a lot of people who've had a lot of fun – to put it mildly – over the years, I got a yen for religion when I was in my forties. The nightclub entrepreneur James Palumbo says that a man should have fun in his twenties, decide on a trade in his thirties, make money in his forties, get political in his fifties and become religious in his sixties, but having lived somewhat of a fast life, I'd got round to the religion bit two decades early.

Typically of me, it wasn't because I was poor or sick or sad, but because I'd just sold my house to a property developer for a very large sum of money. After a lifetime of being in the red – though I had earned a fortune as a writer in my twenties and thirties, I had spent it faster than I banked it, mostly on enough cocaine to cause the entire Colombian army to talk each other to death – I was at last a millionaire. Praise the Lord and pass the poor-box!

My generosity – which had always been well-developed, to the point that beggars frequently chased me down the street yelling 'Oi, love, you've given me too much!' after I had bestowed a cheeky twenty-spot on them – now knew no bounds. Andrew Carnegie's saying 'He who dies rich dies shamed' ringing in my ears, I embarked on a crazed rampage to divest myself of what I couldn't help seeing as my Monopoly money PDQ. And when my accountant pointed out that my actions might soon lead me to join that boozy band of brothers who benefited from my bounty while bedding down in many a shop doorway, I said the first thing that came into my head; 'O hon, I WANT to stop. Really I do! But I'm a – I'm a CHRISTIAN!'

As I said it, I was aware that it was, to some degree, true. I hadn't been to church since my mum died, and I hadn't studied the Bible since Sunday school. But as I said it, it got me thinking. I knew that when I handed over cash to homeless types, I got a strange feeling, a feeling my husband Dan swore that Count Leo 'War And Peace' Tolstoy had also experienced during his dealings with beggars and which had led him to Christianity. I basically believe everything my husband Dan tells me – except if it's to do with the Jews and Israel, neither of which he has a clue about

– so I was well up for this. (Later, regrettably, I would read a different version of this story: one day as he walked down the street, Tolstoy passed a beggar. Reaching into his pocket to give the beggar money, he found that his pocket was empty. Looking at the poor man, Tolstoy said, 'I'm sorry, my brother, I have nothing to give.' To his surprise, the beggar brightened. He said, 'You gave me more than I asked for . . . you called me brother.' Tolstoy, you cheap bastard – you KNOW you were a count!)

But I knew on another level what this feeling was because another boy I'd once believed everything from – Toby Young – had told me the word when I was in my twenties: I was feeling 'oceanic'. This is a psychological term coined by Romain Rolland and popularized by Sigmund Freud to criticize the psychological feeling of religion; according to Rolland's definition of the term, this feeling is the source of all religious energy, a sensation of an indissoluble bond with everything in the world. One can only imagine that Freud didn't care for it as he was rooting for Team Cocaine, which sort of does the same thing, but with nosebleeds and bickering and even quicker bankruptcy.

Whatever it was, it felt WELL good. I didn't know if this was because I was flash, or because, as a hedonist, I appreciated the way the pleasure centre of the brain lights up twice as bright on giving as it does on receiving in some favoured people. (Not all, of course: we all know some sad soul whose apparent role model is Scrooge McDuck and who can't spend 50p on a sachet of Whiskas without thinking 'Hmm – what's in this for me?') Now I was thinking it might be because I was religious – which, let's face, sounds a lot more grown up and noble than flinging money about just for the sheer hedonistic heck of it.

So I began to hang around churches, like I'd once lurked around the houses of people I had crushes on, or drug dealers. (Same thing, usually, in my case.) I must point out here that this wasn't some 'I-was-lost-and-now-I'm-found' sob story. These days, many people reach out to faith 'to find peace'; the way I saw it, I had too much peace in my life already. In faith, I was looking to be troubled. Another difference is that every film and pop starlet, trawling after a reason to exist, says, 'I'm not religious – but I am spiritual' whereas I don't have a spiritual bone in my body. What I am is religious.

But how exactly was this going to express itself, aside from the obvious gestures of philanthropy and volunteer work? (Religious believers carry out a whopping 80 per cent of voluntary work in this country – we're always being told that you don't have to be religious to be a good person but obviously atheists are too busy shopping and sacrificing chickens to Satan to spend any time helping the needy.) My new vicar friend, the Reverend Gavin Ashenden of Sussex University, never said, 'I am a Christian,' but rather 'I'm trying to be a Christian'. Was I supposed to love my neighbour? As we've seen, I've always been fine with that, even to the extent of appropriating a shared swastika from the Indian family next door in Bloomsbury. How about turning the other cheek? Yeah, right!

Also – a bit like Goldilocks – I couldn't find a church that was just right. The first had a vast, magnificent stone interior, which was rather badly offset by the large sign reminding us to KEEP HOLD OF YOUR HANDBAGS AT

ALL TIMES. Was it a test about rich men and needles? Should we actually let go of our handbags and trust in the Lord? I found myself puzzling about this when I should have had my mind on higher things. I decided not to go there anymore when a well-dressed woman shot me a look of pure evil when I put a tenner in the collection plate she had just passed me. I didn't MEAN to make her 50p look risible, FFS! If you can't flash your cash around the poor-box, where CAN you?

Next I tried a smaller church with a lovely female vicar. I was happy there for a few weeks until Harvest Festival, when my friend Sara and I rocked up with a selection of luxury goods for the alms boxes. There was a great deal of eye-rolling and looks which clearly said 'You could have got two dozen Honest Value horse-burgers for the price of them Chocolate Bath Olivers!' Why SHOULDN'T the poor have the best once in a while, we had reasoned. We were amazed when they hid our lovely stuff behind all the Poundland pastries on the display table; was it to do with the sin of pride? Later in the service, a child – not a tot, but around ten, and not just a random passer-by, but a regular attendant – identified the cross as 'a space rocket' and everyone laughed indulgently. Sara and I stared at each other in absolute horror and stormed out to get righteously drunk. (To be fair, I did get my own back by going into this church drunk as a lord in the summer of 2012 and writing in the Guest Book THERE IS NO G-D BUT THE G-D OF THE JEWS. So I can't really complain.)

At the Salvation Army Church, I was similarly disap-pointed. Though I participated in a very enjoyable soup-run to a bunch of charming homeless men on Brighton seafront, I was somewhat put off by the primness of the Army-folk themselves.

'Why can't we sing "Onward Christian Soldiers"?' I inquired after one rather limp, modern service.

'Come now, Julie, it's a bit militaristic!' jollied charming Major Swanson.

'But I have to call you Major, Major, and you wear a military uniform and lead an army!' I replied, not unreasonably. After a tussle with their press officer about the evils of alcohol, I made my excuses and left but not before contributing a cheque for £500 to their appeal for the homeless. 'And if I'd been drunk, it would have been a thousand...' I couldn't help adding over my shoulder as I walked out.

There was also the irksome matter of the Trinity. The sheer ridiculousness of the notion that God would have a child – a little baybee! – struck me as being laughable when I was very young, and as a rebellious teenager the twee nature of the Nativity seemed to sum up the ability of Gentile culture to suck the fun, awe and glory out of everything. I can see the tragedy and drama of the Jesus scenario – he was a half-crazed, self-hating, half-brilliant rabbi – but I still don't buy the basic premise. THE CREATOR DOESN'T HAVE INDIVIDUAL CHILDREN, CLOWNS – WE'RE ALL HIS CHILDREN! Isn't it enough that we've got to drool over 'The Royal Family' like half-wits without making the miracle of Creation into a freaking soap opera too?

A hymn which kept cropping up during my Sunday sojourns ended with the line 'three-in-one', followed by an exclamation mark; no matter how solemn my mood, this

little flourish never failed to raise a snicker, with its irresistible connotations of 'Buy One, Get One Free!' But the
questing camel's back was truly broken when one Sunday (at Space Rocket HQ) we were encouraged to express
our hopes for the coming year. An old guy stood up and
demanded that Christianity should stop stepping on other
religions around the world. Laugh? I almost choked on
my wafer. All across the Muslim world, Christians are tortured, raped and murdered for their faith. Saying sorry
when someone steps on your foot is one thing; apologising
when they are butchering thousands of your co-religionists
each year is taking the English apology reflex a bit too far
for me to swallow, even with a big gulp of Communion
wine.

Why didn't I try to become a Jew, you might ask? I
was surely the only woman ever to watch *Sex And The City*
and not envy Miranda her brains, Samantha her sex life
or Carrie her shoes, but rather Charlotte her conversion.
Well, I was – cringe – SHY. Yes, after all those decades
of stripping off standing on tables while singing 'Hey Big
Spender!' down the Groucho Club, I was still that stunned-
silly ('a tart in a trance', to use my mum's immortal phrase)
teenager when it came to approaching something or someone I really cared about, even at the age of 40. O shyness
– what crimes are committed in thy cowering name, and
what folly triumphs! For instance, if I hadn't been so shy,
I'd have gone and got a synagogue that suited me. Instead
of letting the synagogue least suitable in the world come
and get me...

In the spring of 2009, I got an email from someone
calling herself Rabbi Elizabeth Tikvah Sarah (never trust

anybody with three names – see Lee Harvey Oswald, John Wilkes Booth and Tara Palmer Tompkinson), sympathizing with a newspaper account of my struggles with the ever-lurking handbag-thieves and space-rocket-spotters of the local kirks. Why didn't I come round to her synagogue – or 'shoool', as I always prissily refer to Jewish places of worship – and have a chat? It was called Brighton & Hove Progressive Synagogue – and I've always believed in progress – and even better for a lazy bitch such as myself, IT WAS LITERALLY IN THE NEXT STREET! So one spring afternoon, I put on my most modest dress and my most pious face and got myself around there at a trot.

I needn't have worried about preparing myself, though, because talk about not standing on ceremony! I've been to squat parties that were more formal than the BHPS shul, which at the time I took to be a sign of welcoming friendliness; there was none of that knocking on the door and being turned away three times like what happened to Charlotte in *SATC*. (The 'informality' – some would say sloppiness – of this shul hadn't changed by the summer of 2013 when, during the writing of this book, I went to its website to check up on facts. The History section has two examples of that classic journalistic howler wherein the writer's notes to themselves have been left in – 'In 1992 [check year], after a period when the congregation was led by lay leaders, Rabbi Willie Wolff joined the synagogue, to be followed a few years later in 1995 [check date] by Rabbi Paul Glantz. Since December 2000 the congregation has been led by Rabbi Elizabeth Tikvah Sarah.' Note that no one has to CHECK DATE/YEAR when the rule of Rabbi ETS – or 'Elli', as her flock were rather sickeningly encouraged to call her – began, as that obviously counts as Year Zero.)

The shul itself was located in a rather shabby former school and Call-Me-Elli was a bit too I'm-only-human for my liking (I want to be slightly scared of a rabbi – sad but true) but heck, I was in a synagogue at last! Truth be told, so extreme had my respect and awe for the Jews always been that in all my forty years I had dodged every chance to see inside one that had ever come my way – an attitude, I now realize, which seems eerily close to that of an anti-Semite. (Just thought I'd get that one in to give a cheap thrill to all the 'Aha! PHILO-SEMITISM IS ANOTHER FORM OF ANTI-SEMITISM!' seat-sniffers.)

So anyway, I bunged her the mandatory cheque for a few thousand quid – 'For the roof' I said vaguely: Ruth got off cheaply! – which had by now become my calling card and we sat down for a 'chat'. (Her word. Should have known she was a wrong 'un. I never knowingly met a 'chat' I liked.)

'Is there anything I can do to help here?' I barged right in. 'I mean – cleaning?' Oops – my willingness to perform menial tasks for These People had taken on a parasexual edge perilously early on! 'I mean, anything?' No Lady Muck, I!

Call-Me-Elli laughed, as if I was joking. 'Oh, we have cleaners. The question is, what can we do for YOU?'

I'm always stumped when people ask me this question – probably something to do with being an only child, having a rich inner life, never getting bored with my own company, not having been breast-fed; all that jazz. Was it a trick question? I'd just given her three thousand nicker, FFS! I eyed her suspiciously: 'How d'you mean?'

'Well, would you like to come to the service on Shabbat?'

A shiver went down my spine. OH. MY. GOSH! 'COULD I? I mean, is that POSSIBLE?'

Rabbi Elli (say it fast and it sounds like a crazed Mafia hitman, or perhaps a scheming Venetian puppet-master) laughed, as though humouring a half-wit. 'Of course! Lots of our congregation aren't Jewish.'

Of course, warning bells should have rung then. But I could see the prize – the diamond-encrusted bagel – hanging a mere millimetre from my nose. 'I'd love to!'

I walked out of there on air, and it wasn't just because I was three thousand pounds lighter, either. Saturday came, and back I trotted to the shul where I was greeted by a lovely man who couldn't have been a day over 80, on a mobility scooter. He was, it transpired, the Shul Security.

'Shabbat Shalom,' he smiled.

I all but swooned away to a sliver of shiksa quicksilver on the spot. 'Shabbat Shalom,' I replied, and stepped inside the sanctuary I had sought for so long.

There were no marble floors and crystal chandeliers in that humble building. You could see from bits of the ceiling where gym equipment had hung before the school was a shul – and, as if in mute tribute, I couldn't help notice with a start that several of the congregation were WEARING TRAINERS! But no signs warned you to keep your hand on your ha'penny; no precocious tot mistook the Lord for a hot-air balloon, thus causing chuckles all round. Every male head proudly wore a kippah, and there was AN ACTUAL SCROLL! Tears came to my eyes as it was brought out of its cupboard. The sound of the Hebrew language filled my ears. I didn't understand a word but they were definitely speaking my language. Truly this felt like a Holy Place in a way no church ever had for me. And furthermore, I felt the strangest feeling that I HAD NOT BEEN TRULY ALIVE TILL NOW.

Then the Hebrew stopped and Call-Me-Elli started nattering on in English and it really was standard holier-than-thou stuff. The poncy little sub-title of the BHPS, she explained, was CONGREGATION OF PEACE AND FRIENDSHIP, presumably to differentiate it from the three nearby synagogues which are unashamed CONGRE-GATIONS OF WAR-MONGERING AND HATRED. Then the interfaith dialogue propaganda started. Interfaith, schminterfaith! I'd heard about interfaith meetings way back from a Christian mate, who told me he'd started out with high hopes, being an amiable cove, and stopped going to them because they generally ended with the Muslims telling the Buddhists, Sikhs, Hindus, Christians and the Jews present that they were infidels who would burn in Hell, minus the requisite number of virgins for an Allah-approved orgy.

As my mind wandered, so did my eye. Even though a bit goy-heavy for my liking, the congregation contained about half a dozen undeniable male fitties – 'mitties' – from their teens to their sixties. I began to rank them, reflexively, in reverse order – then tore my eyes away from the most do-able and back to my Torah. How despicable was I! No wonder they separate the sexes in less liberal synagogues. Although, I reflected sadly, with my sexually flexible track record, this would hardly stop me – I'd just rate the broads, instead.

Then Call-Me-Elli stopped nagging about the Palestinians, and the sound of Hebrew filled the air again. Immediately I was back in the room – and it didn't have a bed in it. Just belief in the One Lord. I spoke out with the English translation – 'Hear, O Israel! Adonai is our God! Adonai is One!' – and I meant it. Not three-in-one – not buy-one-get-two-free, as the daft Christians would have it. ONE.

There was no doubt, I thought, as I sat with downcast eyes and shyly waited for the congregation to leave before me, that this religion affected me in a way that Christianity had failed to. Though it was in a very foreign language – not even the same alphabet! – I felt I understood what it was getting at, instinctively. This wasn't the religion of turning the other cheek and getting stomped all over by the nearest bully. This was a religion of fighters. And such interesting women! Deborah the judge and Ruth the rebel and Yael the assassin and Esther the warrior princess; a far cry from the weeping mothers and repentant prossies of the New Testament. And of course Sarah the Mirthful, 'Mother Of The Jews', who laughed when the Lord told her that at the age of ninety she would bear her first child and thus give birth, basically, to Civilization. How typical of milksop Christianity that a cynical old broad had to become an awed young virgin! And how many honour killings did such undue emphasis on virginity give birth to? Discuss THAT in your Interfaith Dialogue...

But whatever my reservations about Call-Me-Elli, I was going to stick at it – this most beautiful and strange of all the beautiful, strange things I had ever encountered. I got up from my seat, swallowed my pride and went to congratulate the rabbi on her sermon.

A few weeks later, my best friend Y and I were standing on the doorstep of the rabbi's house, clutching a couple of bottles of champagne and trying to look casual, like we went for Shabbat dinners at rabbi's houses every night of the week. Y had recently discovered that she was Jewish too – well, there HAD to be a reason why we'd been bezzies for so long, seeing as she didn't drink, didn't take drugs and hadn't had sex this century – and that her mother had been on the Kindertransport from Hamburg to Liverpool. So we were both, for our various reasons, excited about the evening.

I've asked Y for her memories of the evening as she is not only ceaselessly sober, but endlessly unjudgemental, whereas I am...well, NOT is I suppose the best word. It is in the spirit of such clear-eyed recall that I write the following dialogue:

J: *'Didn't we give the rabbi champagne and they opened some home-brewed rubbish instead?'*

Y: *'Yes, two bottles, and they never saw the light of day while we were there.'*

J: *'Didn't the rabbi canoodle with her girlfriend a bit more than was absolutely necessary at what was basically a religious ritual meal?'*

Y: *'Canoodle! It was a bit more than that. They were all over each other – complimenting and hugging and stroking hair and backs. I found it very uncomfortable – I mean, we know they're gay. If you go to a heterosexual dinner party you don't expect the hosts to behave in such a manner – frankly, I was a bit freaked out and thought that you and I were about to be the warm-up act in a lesbian orgy. We were VERY relieved to get away with our clothes on and almost ran to the car; I wouldn't go back there, even with the promise of cheesecake. Talking of which, the cake they did serve was so dry that as I drove you home I said I would have given anything for some cream or custard – and you said you would have happily paid someone to spit on it! That was so funny I nearly wet myself and when I told you, you said "Cheers, but I'd prefer spit!"'*

J: 'And you came to shul with me a few times – what did you think of her sermons?'

Y: 'I came with you three times and I do remem-ber an awful lot of banging on about how it was fine to be gay. Of COURSE it is – we've all chosen to live in Brighton, we KNOW that! But do we need it repeated over and over again during sermons in a synagogue? Also, she wore trainers while giving the sermon, which even though I'm not religious I found disrespectful when everyone else had dressed up for Shabbat. I expect it was her way of showing how funky and cool she is!'

Indeed, Call-Me-Elli HAD told me excitedly that the BHPS

had appeared in a list of COOL SHULS recently, which I'd thought rather a worldly and, may I say, even shallow boast. So far as I could see – takes one to know one – boasting was quite her thing. And as I continued to attend the shul, I soon learnt that when not boasting about being gay and cool, she was – via the scenic route – boasting about how tolerant she was by ceaselessly ramming the merits of Islam down the collective throats of her captive audience.

I thought that when I'd left the Christian church, I'd waved goodbye to Sabbath Stockholm Syndrome, and a religion which would cringingly apologize as Islamism continued to pay the other religions of the world absolutely zero respect. I'd reckoned that as Call-Me-Elli was not only a woman, but a Jew and a homosexual, she would have no time for Islam whatsoever, knowing the terrible persecution of all three groups under Islam – past AND present. It transpired however that she was part of an organization called Salaam Shalom (look how Islam gets in there first, even though Judaism was born centuries before it – typical!), one aim of which is to highlight the similarities between Judaism and Islam. Here are some of her writings on the subject from 2012:

Of course, there are differences between Islam and Judaism. Nevertheless, there are also significant similarities. The word hajj *is connected, etymologically, to the Hebrew,* chag, *teaching us that Hebrew and Arabic are closely related – and also that certain key values and practices are shared...as we have*

already seen, Hebrew and Arabic are cognate lan-
guages, sharing common roots and concepts. This
is most evident in the traditional forms of greeting.
The Hebrew greeting, 'Shalom Aleichem', and Arabic
greeting, 'Salaam Aleikim', our exact equivalents:
both Jews and Muslims say, 'Peace be upon
you'...both Jews and Muslims don't eat pork and
other pig products, and kill their animals for food by
making an incision to the neck.

This was three years after my brush with her, but her song remains the same as it was back in 2009 – tone deaf and way out of tune with reality. Yes, the two religions may have small things in common – but what about the some-what more pressing facts that in Islamic countries, homo-sexuality is illegal (in many, punishable by death), that anyone who wants to leave Islam – whether for another religion or for atheism – is guilty of apostasy and therefore deserving of death, and that Islam's attitude to spirited women is nothing less than murderous. The words of that Hezbollah freak came back to me as I considered this: 'The Jews love life, so that is what we shall take away from them. We are going to win, because they love life and we love death.' He could see it the massive difference between the two religions – why couldn't she? The old phrase 'None so blind as those who will not see' came to mind, and then Jeremiah 5:21 (King James version): 'Hear now this, O foolish people, and without understanding; which have eyes, and see not; which have ears, and hear not.'

By the start of summer I was having a full-blown crisis

of faith; I loved going to shul every Saturday to hear the Hebrew readings from the Torah, which made my soul sing back even though my voice was silent. Call-Me-Elli's insistence on using her pulpit in order to hammer home the joys of Islam, however, had my soul covering its ears and trilling 'LalalanotLISTENING!' How COULD Islam be as a good a religion as Judaism. fearing and loathing spirited women, Jews and gay people the way it does? That was like saying that fascism was as good as socialism, from where I was sitting. (In a pew in the back row of the synagogue, sulking.)

It didn't help that the *Jewish Chronicle* had run my attendance as a big story on their front page on 18 June, 2009:

Outspoken writer and columnist Julie Burchill is taking her support for Israel and Jewish causes to a new level by becoming a Friend of Brighton and Hove Progressive Synagogue – and considering converting to Judaism.

Ms Burchill has been attending Shabbat services for a month and has begun studying Hebrew. 'I first thought about converting when I was 25,' she said. 'I will be 50 next month so it's hardly a flash in the pan. At a time of rising and increasingly vicious antisemitism from both left and right, becoming Jewish especially appeals to me. Added to the fact that I admire Israel so much, it does seem to make sense – assuming of course that the Jews will have me.'

She added that as an ex-Christian, 'It is a great relief not to hear people banging on about the "Baby Jesus" and the "Holy Ghost" and the whole dumbass shebang. There is only one God and He is the Eternal One. I may or may not become a Jew. But I would venture to state, without qualification, that every other alleged "monotheist" believer is living in a dream world. The filthy stain of anti-Semitism which unites Christian and Muslim is based on their pathetic envy of the perfect, enduring faith of the Jews. We/they rock!'

Shul chair Prue Baker said the congregation had welcomed Ms Burchill 'as we welcome all who share our approach to Judaism and wish to be associated with us. We are an inclusive community and have many Friends who may not be Jewish.'

Another congregant confided that 'Julie has told several people that she's enjoying the services. She's amusing and fun to have around but she's keeping a fairly low profile.'

Still, I comforted myself, not an awful lot of people read the *JC*. The next day the phone rang. It was my friend K. 'Have you seen the *Guardian*?'

'That Islam-licking, seat-sniffing rag? Do me a favour!'

'Well, go and get it. You've made the WORLD NEWS section!'

She wasn't joking. There it was in the *Guardian* World

News – JULIE BURCHILL MOVES CLOSER TO JUDAISM. I was somewhat suffering from the sin of pride as I saw the section where this earth-shattering news had been broken to a waiting world, but nevertheless narrowed my eyes suspiciously; didn't that 'moves closer' bit have an unwholesome sexual connotation? The last time I'd heard the phrase it was in that sultry soul song, performed by Phyllis Nelson, the climax of which was all about 'moving your body real close!'

Still, I read on:

Writer and self-confessed Christian Zionist Julie Burchill has deepened her love affair with Judaism by becoming a regular at a Brighton synagogue.

Burchill, who has expressed admiration for Jews on many occasions, has also started taking Hebrew classes at the Brighton and Hove Progressive Synagogue.

According to Rabbi Elizabeth Tikvah Sarah, the columnist has been a regular at Shabbat services for a month and has become a friend of the synagogue. She said that while membership was only for Jews, becoming a friend was open to everyone.

'People become friends because their partners are Jewish but they also join for other reasons. Sometimes it's because they identify with our inclusion and egalitarianism.'

Religious services are conducted in Hebrew and

English, there is an emphasis on gender equality and acceptance of lesbian and gay Jews.

'People come on journeys. Whatever Julie is in the outside world I treat her as an individual on an individual journey.'

I threw the fiendish rag to the floor with a yelp of dismay – once more, the *Guardian* had succeeded in ruining a perfectly nice day for me, which I had come to believe was their main mission in life ever since, in the days when I was under contract to them, my commissioning editor would know PRECISELY the day when I had a literally incapacitating hangover and would cheerily call at nine demanding two thousand words by noon. (Though come to think of it, with my drinking schedule, he WAS sort of spoilt for choice.)

But THIS took the biscuit. I was on a JOURNEY, was I! Well, that was news to ME, because I hadn't REALIZED that I'd been going to sodding *X-Factor* auditions every Saturday. All that time I believed I'd been going to the House of the Lord (albeit a bit of a scabby one) to praise Him – when in reality I'd been there to Nail It, Own It and Make It Mine. AND Call-Me-Elli had managed to get the gay stuff in the shop window again! All in all, she made my Shabbat sojourns sound like a cross between a Simon Cowell talent show and a Gok Wan scream-fest.

How public was this thing going to get? And JUST at the moment when I was really thinking hard about my future attendance at the shul, too. Suddenly I knew how poor Diana Spencer must have felt, as she attempted to evade a loveless marriage at the eleventh hour, and was told by her older sisters 'Too late, Duch – your face is on the tea towels.'

It shows how rare philo-Semitism is that even a minor figure such as myself – a drunken hack past her best, no less – could cause such a kerfuffle. Not content with putting me on their front page, the *JC* now started up an online poll asking whether or not I should convert – fair enough, Call-Me-Elli had announced that I was on a Journey and now in true TV talent show tradition the public would have their say. By 22 June, 60% were for conversion, Cheryl Cole was crying and Louis Walsh was telling me I reminded him of a Gentile Roseanne Barr. Just to rub it in, the *JC* reported, 'It has been the most read story on this site so far this week and was followed up by several other newspapers, including the *Guardian* and a number of bloggers.'

Very well. I'd stick it out a bit longer, but I'd stand my ground and make my objections known in the way I always had since I figured out as a teenager that speech was my second language. I'd write about what I liked and disliked about My Journey. And let THAT go to deadlock...

In the *JC* of 23 July, I had a fun little piece headlined SHE'S TWIGGED: MACCA HAS A THING FOR JEWS in which I made light of the recent unpleasantness between Paul McCartney and his out-going wife:

So Heather Mills has claimed that 'some of my best friends are Jewish'. You want to believe her, don't you? If ever anyone could benefit from the warm hearts and cool judgement of my favourite ethnic stereotypes, it's poor old Heather, who makes the

Whore of Babylon look like Aung San Suu Kyi when it comes to securing a place in public esteem.

The problem is, this claim is on the same level of credibility as it might be if she had stated: 'I taught Susan Boyle how to sing' or 'I invented toast.'

Yes, our Brighton correspondent – not me! – recently went to take a peek at the new vegan cafe she's started up down here in Sodom-on-Sea and, on mentioning that she was Jewish, was surprised to be told by Miss Mills that – literally! – some of her best friends were Jewish. And that she had applied to have some of the food sold at the joint approved by the Beth Din. Even though it's going to be open on a Saturday...

Nothing much THERE for Call-Me-Elli to get her trainers in a twist about, you'd think. But I went on...

Opinion in some quarters is that the very Gentile Mills has finally twigged that her ex has a thing for Jewish chicks – Linda Eastman, Nancy Shevell – and is doing the next best thing to converting – going kosher by association – in an effort to tempt him back. Do me a favour! Why in the name of heck would a semi-fit woman of 41 (or is it 21 this week? – I can never keep up) in possession of a sizeable fortune want to set her cap – kippah, even! – at a 67-year-old geezer? She's got what she wanted!

I hate to say it, but it's creepy how much Sir Paul and I have in common. We're both old, rich, live in Brighton and Hove, dye our hair, have somewhat eccentric exes – and like Jews! And when I say 'like', I mean it in the biblical sense – as in 'begat'. Except, hopefully, without the actual begatting. At Sir Paul's age, or even mine, that would tip the inclination from quirky to just plain weird.

Some people – and wouldn't THEY be a whole bunch of fun at a house party! – think it's bad to fancy one ethnic group more than another. But presumably they don't think it's bad for straight people to just fancy the opposite sex, or for gay people to just fancy the same one. If that isn't discrimination – writing off half the human race as a lousy lay – then what is?

Leave us challah-chasers to our innocent appreciation of an ancient and noble people, I say. At a time when Islam-licking on the part of oddball infidels is rife, I'm damned if I'm going to apologise for fancying Sacha Baron Cohen or Scarlett Johansson. We all make choices every day – and I choose the Chosen.

I haven't been a hack for three hundred years without learning a few little tricks of the trade. Without naming her, I'd given the old one-two to Call-Me-Elli's twin obsessions – the OK-ness of gayness and the equal merit of

Islam. And didn't she just notice, too! Next day at shul she was far from her usual everything-is-beautiful/I'd-like-to-buy-the-world-a-kosher-Coke mode. No sooner had the beautiful Hebrew prayers come to an end than she was in like Flynn, banging on about how one faith was as good as another, and sounding even more banal than usual – which was going some. Then she drew herself up to her full height – hard to calculate, as I had come to look down on her so much already – and pronounced 'We must be vigilant about the rubbish we talk – and the rubbish we write!'

Come on, of COURSE she meant me. Who else was a professional writer there? She wasn't referring to people who were keen diarists, obviously: 'Deer Diary, I hate the Profit and his beard, TRUE!' But I've always liked the description 'a cool customer' and as I studied my prayer-book, I was determined to keep my temper under control.

The sermon ended and, as usual, I waited politely for all the Jews (and the fake ones, I reflected bitterly, THE FAKE ONES LIKE ME who made up such a large part of the congregation – giving the rabbi's bigging-up of Islam an even more sinister spin, come to think of it...) to file out before I did. Then I walked straight up to Call-Me-Elli, looked her straight in the eye, put out my hand and said, 'Interesting sermon, rabbi!'

She took my hand and shook it. She looked quite shocked: 'You're very open-minded Julie!'

'Yes, yes, I am,' I smiled graciously. I dropped her hand and walked out of the shul for the last time, seething.

You absolute, ocean-going COW, I thought to myself as I stomped home. I wish I'd asked to see the receipt for the 'roof-mending' cheque I gave you. I bet you spent that money on taking your girlfriend to Lesbos...

'I avoided writers very carefully because they can perpetuate trouble as no one else can,' wrote F. Scott Fitzgerald in *The Crack-Up*; as with most things writers write about writers, this was a heads-up more than a put-down, I thought to myself as I proceeded to tell the tale of my fast-mo hissy-fest at the BHPS to anyone who'd listen. The Season of Goodwill arrived in what seemed like no time after my July swansong at shul, and I took this happy opportunity to further distance myself from my cradle Christianity by sticking the boot in to Call-Me-Elli and all who sailed with her on the SS Stockholm Syndrome. In the *JC* of 9 December, I wrote:

Earlier this year, I did something I had dreamed of since I was a child growing up in the very gentile English West Country; I attended a synagogue. After a few months, I stopped. It wasn't them, it was me.

When I finally plucked up my courage and walked into a local synagogue for the first time, I was pleased to feel a sense of extreme excitement and tranquility...but, after a few weeks, the trouble started. The exciting Torah readings about God smiting the enemies of the Israelites were followed by earnest sermons on the benefits of multi-faith dialogue.

All across the Muslim world, Christians are raped, tortured and murdered for their faith. Let me make this clear. I'm not looking for a religion that stomps all over other religions. But I am looking for a religion that stands up for itself, and for others who are in a – raped, tortured, murdered – position where they are unable to do so. Like I said, it's not you, it's me.

But as the Season of Goodwill wore on, so did my contrarian nature rev up, and on 22 December, *JC* readers were treated to the following:

This will be my last JC column for a year or so as I feel I have said all I can say for the time being about my abiding affection and reverence for the Chosen, both here and in their beautiful homeland. You should know that the reason I'm stepping away for a while has nothing to do with the hysterical levels of abuse that greet any Gentile who expresses support for Israel; on the contrary, I very much enjoy a bit of a verbal scrap. But don't get me wrong, my admiration for the Jews and Israel came first; the nasty name-calling is just a side benefit.

I've had some times since I started this column. I began attending a shul, and took the first steps towards converting to Judaism, then threw in the towel on both. Basically, I don't go to a synagogue on a Saturday morning to be preached at about how Islam is the equal of Judaism, and yet that's what I got the last time I was there – from a female, gay rabbi, already! I'd love to see her walk into a mosque and tell the worshippers that Judaism was the equal of Islam, that women should be just as able to be preachers as men and that homosexuality is every bit as valid a personal choice as heterosexuality.

I wonder how many minutes she'd last? Which makes my point completely: an intolerant religion is not the equal of a tolerant religion. And to say that it is, is surely pretzel logic of the most twisted kind.

I have witnessed the self-loathing Stockholm Syndrome of what my hero Howard Jacobson fingered in his Booker Prize-winning The Finkler Question *as the ASHamed Jews, and came to the conclusion that it wasn't a Jew that I wanted to be so much as a Zionist. And I can do this by helping to buy fire engines for frontline Israeli towns like Sderot, and by donating a good whack of cash each year to send care parcels to lone IDF soldiers – and still stay in bed with my husband of a Saturday without having to schlep off to a shul and receive lectures on the wonders of Islam.*

All in all, I thought I'd been quite clement, so imagine my surprise when I was told that one 'Jess Wood' had brought a complaint against me to the Press Complaints Council. Ooo, I thought, I've heard that name before. Of course I had – she was ONLY Call-Me-Elli's 'better half' (not difficult, all things considered), the partner-in-petting during that fateful Shabbat dinner which my friend Y had feared would turn into a full-on Sapphic free-for-all.

Craftily, she hadn't taken issue with the stuff about her missus; instead – very offensively, to my mind, given the ever more monstrous development of the persecution – she had claimed that my claim that Christians are persecuted 'all across the Muslim world' was inaccurate and misleading. What a rotten thing to do, and how against the loving, inclusive Judaism which her blow-hard bird banged on so much about – forgiving the bully, forgetting the victim.

But the sensible and savvy Press Complaints Commission were having none of it. In February 2010, they ruled that care had been taken to ensure such 'robust opinions' had sufficient basis in fact. Because, of course

The commission emphasized that the Code permits newspapers to present subjective independent comment, provided any opinion is clearly distinguished from fact...on this occasion, the article was written in the first person and was clearly identifiable as the columnist's personal experience of religion. Readers generally would not have been misled into believing there were no alternative views to the one presented by the author.

The article contained the columnist's reaction to a claim that Christianity steps on the toes of other religions. She stated: 'All across the Muslim world,

Christians are tortured, raped and murdered for their faith'. The newspaper accepted that this was a generalization but had substantiated the statement by providing examples of areas (such as Sudan, Indonesia, Iraq and northern Nigeria) where the dominant religion is Islam and Christian groups had suffered persecution. It had also supplied various news articles that reported incidents of Muslim violence against Christians.

No breach of clause 1 (Accuracy) had been established by the complainant.

I might have fallen away even with a different rabbi – who knows? But Call-Me-Elli didn't make it difficult to give up easily.

It was partly that I find it hard to stick at any discipline, being bone-idle and highly hedonistic (for instance, I was only a lesbian for six months), and I realized that Judaism was such an extraordinarily complex and rich religion that I would really have to commit to do it properly. As I can't even commit to *Lost* or any of those long American television shows, this seemed unlikely. But the rabbi's insistence that all religions were equally wonderful were not just increasingly hollow but actively offensive to me in the face of the growing intolerance and bigotry of Islam – as I write this, in August 2013, two teenage Jewish girls from North London have just been brought back to Britain by air ambulance after having acid thrown on their faces and chests by two men on a motorcycle, in Zanzibar (where they were working in an orphanage as volunteers) after one of them was attacked by a woman for the supreme sin of singing in the street during Ramadan.

Not only was the PCC on my side, but I received many emails from rabbis in Brighton and all over London, inviting me to try their shuls instead, as well as commiserations from many Jews. I found the following message from Stanley Victory particularly affecting:

> It saddens me to read that you have given up with attending synagogue and converting to Judaism. I can see how you would be put off after what you have experienced. You are not alone. I am a Jew who attends a Liberal Synagogue and I too feel put off sometimes. So do many others that I know.
>
> There are times that I leave synagogue on Shabbat feeling frustrated and angry rather than at peace and happy.
>
> I know that the rabbi that you are referring to is Elizabeth Tikvah Sarah. You will find her name in the 'About Us' section of the Jews for Justice for Palestinians website of which she is a signatory among a few other 'progressive' rabbis. On the 27th of this month, there will be a protest vigil in front of the Israeli Embassy where according to Jews for Justice for Palestinians 'Between 27 December 2008 and 18 January 2009, over 1,400 Palestinians were killed by Israel in a brutal and illegal attack on the Gaza Strip, destroying lives and infrastructure'.

They will be there alongside Palestine Solidarity Campaign who believe that all of Israel is illegitimate and that 'from the river to the sea' is all Palestine. Their goal is the destruction of Israel. Why our Liberal 'leaders' choose to stand with those that wish our destruction just does not make sense.

They seem to have an obsession with Islam. I sometimes wonder why they don't just convert and be done with it. Interfaith is fine, but how about mingling with other Jews once in a while too? Some of the organizations that they have interfaith with have been documented to be anti-Semitic. Earlier this year, many of the congregation of a Liberal Synagogue walked out of their Rosh Hashannah service when Danny Rich decided to spend most of the time talking about the wonders of Islam and the Moslem holiday of Eid.

To support Israel in Liberal Judaism feels taboo. Why don't I leave? Believe me, there are times that I really do think about it. I stay because I am a progressive Jew and I and believe women have equal rights. I support Women of the Wall, I don't care what colour you are, what your sexuality is or how you want to practise Judaism, but I am not interested in Islam or anti-Israel propaganda. I can understand that people in Liberal Judaism want to question Israel, but there are those that cross the line and support their own enemies. They are supporting their own destruction with their alliances.

I want to go to synagogue and learn about Judaism, I want to buy Israeli olive oil. I get jealous when I learn of other branches of Judaism saying prayers for the IDF, why can't we? When they have an Israeli flag at other synagogues, why can't we? Why can't our trips to Israel be about our Jewish heritage? Where is the pride?

I stay in hope that things will change, that the Rabbis will listen to their congregation, that they will be real supporters of Israel and will stop shoving Islam down our throats. Danny Rich has been appointed to five more years as Chief Executive. Maybe I am the one that is naive?

Julie, don't let your experience at that synagogue put you off. As I am sure you know, not all synagogues are that way. There is also Reform, Masorti and Orthodox. Don't give up. You are an inspiration and a mensch, we would be quite happy to have you.

But after the Lord Mayor's Show...soon I was receiving a multitude of emails from the rabbi's girlfriend (whose email was, rather appallingly, 'Jess Kangaroo') who did a complete U-turn on the New Way To Be A Jew shtick by coming on like the most preposterous stereotype of a yenta – meddler, gossiper, meddlesome, busybody, nuisance, to quote the Urban Dictionary – I'd ever come across. One line actually said 'We asked you into our home – and this is how you repay us!' I wish I'd answered, 'I gave your bird two bottles of champagne and three thousand pounds "for the roof" – and this is how you repay ME, with home-brew and complaints to the PCC!' Eventually the messages petered out, until just before Christmas 2012 when I received an email from Jess Kangaroo, hopping mad about something I'd written about transsexuals picking on women, telling me I'd lost my moral compass and suggesting that I could learn a valuable lesson from the John Lewis commercial currently being shown on TV. This, really, said it all to me about the intellectual calibre of Call-Me-Elli and her crew – a cool 34 centuries of rabbinical wisdom to choose from, and Miss Kangaroo suggests that I will find insight in a short commercial featuring a bad cover of a Frankie Goes To Hollywood song and a pretend snowman making a great effort to buy another snowman a hat. Perfect! I may not have found any degree of spiritual enlightenment from my association with BHPS – but that email definitely gave me one of the best laughs I had in the whole of 2012.

TEN

UNCHOSEN

My 24 December 2011 horoscope, as foretold by Claire Petulengro in the *Brighton Argus*, read as follows: 'Make sure you're mixing with the right crowd this Christmas Eve or you are going to end up getting yourself a reputation. Could it be that you're looking to get a reaction? It would appear so.'

A bit late to start worrying about that now, I smirked to myself as I fastened my snood around my hair with my Zionist Federation pin and nipped out to celebrate the start of Chanukah in Palmeira Square, Hove. As I walked with my Hebrew teacher, my Jewish best friend, my Jewish goddaughter and my half-Jewish son towards the modest menorah, the huge, opulent Christmas tree on the other side of the square seemed to mock my very un-Jewishness. 'Come on, darlin' – get over here and get drunk!' it seemed to twinkle, evilly. 'It's not really you, is it – standing about stone cold sober, singing songs in a language you don't understand, with a bunch of people so respectable they literally couldn't get arrested if they tried...'

And it had a point, as trees go. For starters, how could

an unrepentant old lush like me ever dream she could become a Jew? Let's face it, I don't just like to have a glass of wine and relax, I don't just like to sip at a single malt whisky. I like to get drunk, and expensively so. Surely I started to dislike Call-Me-Elli at the moment she substituted her homebrew for my Veuve Clicquot, if I'm being honest? Or was it during the first after-service get-together, when we had been served that awful sweet Jewish wine in tiny plastic cups, which I had knocked back in one, like a shot, before looking around eagerly for more, recalling the line someone said about the food somewhere – prison? hospital? – 'It's horrible and there's not enough of it.'

(Happily the same cannot be said for Israeli vino; I've always laughed at people who say breakfast is the most important meal of the day, but when you take it in the swaggering sunshine of the Tel Aviv or Eilat seafront and it features a Cosmopolitan and a bottle of Yarden white, I'm starting to think they might have something.)

I remember the waitress in the Herzliya branch of Moses Restaurant when I ordered a bottle of wine for a table of four, 'What are we celebrating?' How I laughed! But the other three didn't; they were Jews, and a bottle of wine between four seemed somewhat sailor-on-shore-leave to them, too. In her great Tel Aviv novel, *When I Lived In Modern Times*, Linda Grant has a character say: 'He told us about an Irgun terrorist under sentence of death. Someone brought him a bottle of brandy and after three weeks he'd finished it. According to the Jews, that made him an unreliable alcoholic.'

But I AM an unreliable alcoholic; even so, as

metaphors go, the place where I live would get laughed out of town if I stuck it in a novel – between a synagogue and a church, forever in limbo between the culture I was born to and the culture I crave. 'Why are you doing this – siding with the Jews all the time?' Charles Saatchi asked me once, almost angrily. 'Do you really need to go looking for trouble that much?' Maybe. I still can't read my Torah, and I got burned by my menorah; the sober, wholesome families gathered in Palmeira Square were far from being my natural constituency.

A Jewish friend, the brilliant writer Emma Forrest, once observed me drinking Jack Daniel's from the bottle while watching *Big Brother* and singing to my cat. She stared, deadpan, then said 'Wow – you really are a Gentile, aren't you! I forget sometimes...' I don't. And while I didn't mind much being a bad Christian, it would break my black little heart to be a bad Jew, hence my reluctance to re-engage with the Jewish religion. I find rules to live by in general hard to deal with, despite repeated proof that they exist for a good reason – only last month, for instance, my friend and fellow Gentile Karl and I went straight from our Hebrew class to a restaurant where we proceeded to scoff oysters like heathens just coming off of a hunger strike. And – serve us right – we were VERY sick the next day. But having very little working knowledge of cause and effect, I'm sure I'll do it again. Though I haven't consciously ordered pig-meat in more than five years, I watch my husband like a hawk when he's eating it, and grab any leftovers with the risibly self-righteous excuse that, 'It would be disrespectful to the pig to leave it on the plate – it would mean he died in vain!' Yes, I KNOW...

On the subject of trespasses, might I just take this opportunity to apologize to any Jews who I have liked against their will? There's the odd voice here and there which pours scorn on devotion to my chosen team, but these are as often as not strange characters (Gilad Atzmon, my late mother-in-law). I leave it to the Jewish people themselves to agonize over their future; I choose only to see the good side of them, and I see this as a perfectly honourable antidote – a rational act, even – to centuries of genocidal cruelty on the part of non-Jews towards Jews.

You'd think that with the world being the way it is, there are worse things than being adored. I'll say sorry, anyway, and also to any Jews who, even worse than liking them, object to me FETISHIZING them, in the words of David Baddiel in the *Sunday Times*. I would like to assure David Baddiel, in particular, that there is not the LEAST danger of me EVER fetishizing him – especially sexually, as the word implies: frankly, I'm more likely to be found fetishizing a dead, decapitated dog. I should, in the interests of complete candour, say that Mr Baddiel and I have history – accent on the hiss, as in hissy-fit on his part – and I'll reveal it now, as it shows that even though I admire the Jews greatly as a people, I'm certainly not some sadsack who goes around sucking up to people just because they're Jews. Unlike the likes of Galloway, Livingstone and the Islam-licking monstrous regiments of the media, who frequently suck up to the nastiest type – gynophobic, homophobic, racist – of mullah or dictator, just because he is a Muslim and can therefore be relied upon to be instinctively anti-American.

In the closing weeks of the 20th century, a waiting

world reeled when the alleged droll – Baddiel – published his second novel, *Whatever Love Means*. I'd already crossed him years back; Emma Forrest, then a teenage comedy-nut, told me that there was this brilliant new act called Newman and Baddiel – one of them was Jewish and one of them was very keen on my writing and wanted to meet me. Cruelly, she knew I would assume that the beautiful one – Newman, who liked me – was also the Jew, and she said it was an absolute picture to see my face drop when I found out that my beautiful fan was a Gentile, and his less attractive mate the Hebrew. I can't BELIEVE I wrote this, though, in the *Guardian* in 2000 – 'The US has done, is doing and will do more damage to this planet than Nazi Germany, fascist Japan and David Baddiel put together.' SHAME ON ME. And no wonder he sued me, giving the damages to the Holocaust Educational Trust.

But once you've crossed someone once, you may as well make a day of it, so true to form I dived right in:

It's sad, really. Baddiel was one half of Newman and Baddiel, the comic duo who in the early part of the decade became the first jokers (not counting the Eurythmics) to fill Wembley Stadium with screaming hormones. Their fortunes since the split tell a tale of our times' tragic predilection for mediocrity over merit. One of them, Robert Newman (my one-time best friend who I fell violently out with four years ago and haven't spoken to since, so obviously I'm not biased) was a breathtakingly beautiful, incandescently sensitive working-class foundling who made it to Cambridge but left after a nervous break-down; David Baddiel, less glamorously, was a middle-class public schoolboy who went to Cambridge because, well, that's what one does.

As one whose beauty has fled, I won't do much in the way of finger-pointing at Mr Baddiel except to say that when you saw the two of them together, Baddiel didn't look so much like Newman's partner as like his afterbirth, which some short-sighted surgeon had foolishly failed to sever.

Yet Newman's writing career – he wrote two excellent novels, Dependence Day *and* Manners *– has faltered while Baddiel's has thrived. A lot of this can be put down to the public's unswerving love of bad writing. (We are, never forget, the country that made Jeffrey Archer a millionaire for the second time.) Line one, page one, reminds us just how bad Baddiel can be – 'Vic fucked her first the day Princess Diana died.' Is that first before everyone else fucked her, or first before he fucked everybody else? Why not 'Vic first fucked her the day Princess Diana died'? Not, God forbid, that we should be mellifluous or concise. The lads at* Loaded *might not like it!*

And from then on, as the great Victor Lewis-Smith once said of our hero's television show, things go from Baddiel to worrsiel. Predictably, he takes the golf club bore view that the mourning over the death

*of the Princess of Wales was really rather silly (i.e.
female); disgustingly, he uses the word 'fascism' to
describe the mood of supposedly enforced grief, and
on one page he uses it in this context no less than five
times. But if what happened in London in the September of 1997 was fascism, what word can we use
to describe what happened in Germany in the 1930s?*

Again going from Baddiel to worrsiel, I also don't care,
of course, for all those squawking Semitic turkeys who
choose Christmas by dissing Israel – most of them luvvies
– and feel that they must surely suffer from the most eye-
watering level of self-loathing – a somewhat foreign emo-
tion to me, but obviously a very real one. In *Ava Gardner:
The Secret Conversations*, the great film star tells her con-
fidante, the journalist Peter Evans:

*Artie (Shaw, the bandleader, her second husband)
was very conscious of being a Jew...he was at a posh
Hollywood dinner party when they started talking
about Jews. It turned out they were all anti-Semitic.
He said he sat there in silence for a while – apparently nobody knew he was a Jew – then he joined
in with their snide remarks about Jews. He said he'd
never forgive himself for his cowardice.*

When I see Jews sucking up to Islamist organizations
which without doubt despise them, and would eliminate
them without a moment's hesitation, I think of poor Artie
Shaw. As I do when I read about Jews who claim they're

not Jews, as did Cosmo Landesman in the *Sunday Times* in August 2013:

> *I'm just not very Jewish. Jews are smart and successful...Jews are cool....we got brains, wit and looks. Who in their right mind wouldn't want to belong to the tribe? Me. I'm not smart or cool. Even my former Gentile girlfriend [a lie: it was I, his former Gentile wife, who said this, but then Mr Landesman and the truth have always been on vaguely the same terms of familiarity as Israel and Iran] used to say 'How the hell did I end up with the one poor, dumb Jew in London?' Why should I get the kudos of being Jewish when I haven't done anything to deserve it? So if I don't want to be Jewish, what do I want? I want to be a good dad, a good citizen and a decent human being – and great in bed.*

Good luck with that, mate – but really, might it not be marginally less ambitious to aim at being Chief Rabbi?

So of course I don't like ALL Jews – because then I'd have to like an ex-husband, and that way lies lunacy. I also have very little time for Jewish Greens, those strange beasts (another variation on Turkeys For Christmas, come to think of it) who on moving into – or more likely, being born into – an elevated tax bracket immediately forget all the terrible things that happened to Jews in traditional, non-urban, non-capitalist societies, and begin to yearn for them. As I've written, I never tired of reminding my second husband when he came over all misty-eyed about Ye

Goode Olde Dayes that, as a Jew – whether he wanted
to be one or not! – he'd very likely be chasing a skinny
chicken through a shtetl, pursued by Cossacks on horse-
back with whips rather than sitting around pontificating
and pursuing Gentile poontang, and I see no reason to
say anything different about the likes of Zac Goldsmith or
David de Rothschild. Modern Jews are by nature urban,
super-bright and self-made, the opposite of Green. So
what happened to them? When one's family makes their
pile, does their rich (dim) side take over from their Jewish
(smart) side and simply render them as dumb as most
other beneficiaries of inherited wealth of all creeds and
cultures? It seems to me extraordinary for a British or
indeed a European Jew to be dewy-eyed about the good
old days, which would have seen them barred from further
education, amongst other evils. And let's never forget that
the Nazi Party was the first political party to cleave to
Green principles.

But surely a Jew who goes Green is nowhere near as
weird as a Jew who converts to Islam. A *Daily Mail* gossip
item in April 2013 made a waspish point about Jemima
Goldsmith, brother of Zac:

> *The* New York Times *slipped up when it reported on
> Jemima Khan and the Chipping Norton set David
> Cameron and Rebekah Wade belong to, and has pub-
> lished this correction: 'An article about the British
> social scene near Chipping Norton misspelled the
> surname of a writer and socialite. She is Jemima
> Khan, not Kahn.'*

Big difference. Khan is a Muslim name (she was married to Pakistani politician Imran Khan and converted to Islam). Kahn is a traditional Jewish name (from Cohen).

I suspect Jemima would have preferred it if the high-minded Times *had apologised for calling her a socialite.*

The oppression of women has never stopped Westerners such as Khan, Lauren Booth and Yvonne Ridley cosying up to Islam. The excellent Caitlin Moran fingered Jordan as 'Vichy France with tits' in her book *How To Be A Woman*, but how much more this applies to the political equivalent of those strange women who write love letters to serial killers.

Nevertheless, I remain an unrepentant philo-Semite, a love that gets stronger through the years. What started out as me siding with a bunch of outsiders has, as I grow into myself, become the comfort of confidence, in both myself and in the growing strength of the Jewish state.

Would we rare and precious creatures exist without the precedent of anti-Semitism? I like to think so. But we are indeed blessed by the unsurpassable stupidity of our polar opposites.

Phillip Mark McGough – the cleverest man I know – wrote to me:

Anti-Semitism is first and foremost a protest against talent, an objection to a level playing field. It's unique inasmuch as it's the only racism which is also a com-

prehensive ideology, a prefabricated world-view in its own right – many forms of racism are ideological, but only anti-Semitism offers a complete political cosmology, a universal explanation for every woe. It is extraordinarily persistent and Promethean. Anti-Semitism has always been a double-bind. The Jews are accused of every conceivable mutually-exclusive set of vices, often simultaneously and with no sense of contradiction. The Jew is an agitator and fer-menter of revolution; but the Jew is also arch-cap-italist and wire-puller of the established order; the Jew is cowardly and craven and won't fight for his country; but the Jew (or Israeli) is also bloodthirsty and militaristic; the Jew is primitive and his religion a relic superstition; but the Jew is also the harbinger of modernity with all its woes and the Jewish mind the mainspring of dangerous world-shaking ideas.

Anti-Semitism can be as in-your-face as smashing up syn-agogues – a practice which has increased massively, along with the desecration of Jewish graves since 9/11; typically, in true The-Jews-Did-It! tradition, there was proportion-ally a bigger rise in anti-Jewish than in anti-Muslim hate crimes afterwards. But it can also be sly, sneaky, subtle and sometimes surreal. It must, in my opinion, go some way to explaining why Israeli human rights issues are so obsessively concentrated on, while many Arab and African countries are allowed to treat their citizens with as much subhuman sadism as they wish – the pregnant, raped women so frequently sentenced to death by stoning under Islamic regimes come immediately to mind, but the list is never-ending.

In having one human rights rule for democratic Israel – which can be summed up as 'Be perfect or we'll come down on you like a ton of bricks' – and another for the dictatorships which surround it – 'Do what you like to your people – it's your culture!' – Whitey displays an interestingly sly bit of anti-Semitism which is also rather insulting to the said dictatorships and the people they lord it over. The Jews are seen to be the one ethnic group who 'pass' as white; their insistence on making their state a democracy is also seen as a sign of their stubborn refusal to act the savage to Whitey's civilizing influence. And so, conversely, they must be punished for refusing to know their place; it's like the way the French are nastier to those foreigners who try to speak French than they are to those who don't even bother to try. 'You want to act the white man, sonny, you'd better be word perfect or we'll 'ave you round to Amnesty International quicker than you can say intifada! You darkies, though – you do what you like because, face it, you don't know any better, do ya? Bless!'

In short, the Lord forbid that any ethnic group should ignore the all-important world dominance hierarchy and dare to turn from victim into victor – and that is Israel's ultimate crime.

So I no longer go to shul, or even dream of it, but on Shabbat I have my Jewish moment anyway – or rather my two hours, between one and three of an afternoon, outside the Ecostream shop in Brighton. It's here that I experience first-hand my belief that whereas other forms of racism are fading with each generation, in a grotesque way anti-Semitism has recruited new blood through the medium of anti-Zionism. In my own adopted hometown – free'n'funky Brighton – I see it.

Every Saturday now, for a year, our side – black, white, straight, gay, Christian, Jewish, atheist – wave Israeli, English and rainbow flags, sing Hebrew songs, laugh, gossip and demonstrate for the right of Jewish shops to go about their lawful business; their side – blindingly white and bourgeois – scream hate in our faces and demand that the Jewish business closes down. (Where did I hear THAT before?) In the summer of 2013, one of the pro-Hamas matrons mocked my comrade's strong South London accent – it was vile, but somehow satisfying; Nick Cohen's *What's Left?* made sickening, smug, middle-class flesh.

There are always a few Orthodox women there, in ravishing wigs; they smoke like schoolgirls, and stare down the haters insouciantly. One of them says she hears I am going back to Israel soon; if she gives me a couple of empty hummous tubs, can I get her some sand from the beaches of Israel, as they use it in Jewish burial rituals and are running low. All the things I've ever been asked to do – the good, the bad and the ugly, all pleasurable in their own way – pale into insignificance beside this. I nod, unable to speak. I go home, and insist to my husband that we order in a vast Chinese takeaway – the things I do for Israel. Seeing my cabin-sized suitcase, he finds it highly amusing that half of my packing is plastic takeaway containers. On the beach at Tel Aviv, Karl finds it equally amusing to watch me stowing away the golden stuff as though I was planning to clean up on e-Bay. Once my love of the Jews consisted of drawing a line in the sand; now I actually get to steal it back for them.

Another way I stay connected to my magnificent obsession is through learning Hebrew. I can't remember, with the exception of my current marriage, ever sticking at anything that didn't pay the rent, from stamp-collecting to Sapphism. But after three years of weekly lessons, I am the proud boaster of an Ivrit reading age of six, though I fear that might be nearer to an English six-year-old than an Israeli one. Once a week, Karl and I meet at my flat – 'Shalom!' I call through the intercom – 'Shalom!' he calls back: sometimes it's the postman, who once answered 'I'm not Sharon!' – and await 'Miss', our *morah* – Mrs Yael Breuer of Rehovot, Israel, now happily resident in Brighton, who has the face of a Madonna (the kind first one reproduced in a million paintings, not the scary second one) and the patience of a saint as – week in, week out – she listens to me commit GBH on her beautiful native language.

'Isn't it, seriously, quite offensive to you the way I manage to mangle Ivrit so thoroughly?' I emailed her.

'No!' she wrote back.

I've been touched and impressed by your enthusiasm and commitment. You have already excelled at mastering the art of requesting, very fluently, yayin and bira! Even though most people in Israel speak English to a degree, and one can definitely get by with English when visiting Israel, the process of learning the language will gradually give you a real insight to so many aspects of Israeli characteristics, temperament and milieu. Hebrew is a fascinating language that combines its biblical basis with invented modern-day living terms in a way that no other language does.

It doesn't hurt that Yael Breuer is *yafa meod* and that my friend Karl Henry is a *motek* beyond the call of duty. *Anachnu levalot harbeh veh lomedet* – we have fun and learn, which for someone who started playing truant mostly to avoid German lessons at secondary school (the irony!) is a miracle in itself. Why would I ever want to learn another language, I always reasoned, when SPEECH is my second language anyway?

But who knew it could be such a laugh, with a *morah* like Miss and a *motek* like Karl? Yael told me,

It's rewarding to see you both progress, chatting in Hebrew and even making jokes in the language that only a couple of years ago was completely foreign to you. I have taught Hebrew for many years, have had an interesting variety of students and have enjoyed teaching it, but the lessons with you two are quite different. I don't recall any students before who, for example, became involved with deep psychological analysis (in Hebrew!) of the fictional characters illustrated in the text book, to the extent that we now 'know' everything about their family troubles,

alleged drug use and dark secrets. No other student
of mine has ever, after being assigned a homework
task to write a short story or a dialogue, created
a made-up Hebrew singing pop group called the
Lesbo-Tots who proceeded to become a regular fea-
ture in other homework assignments. Similarly, in
all the years I have taught Ivrit, I never thought that
Morrissey would become a regular 'guest' in our
Hebrew lessons, arguing (in Hebrew, of course)
about diets, animal rights and lifestyle. It is not just
fun – you are touchingly emotional about Israel, the
history of the Jewish People and occasionally become
tearful when a new word or phrase relates to a sig-
nificant event or person. I am touched by your and
Karl's genuine loyalty and interest.

Ani rotsa, meaning 'I want', highlights the impatience and, to the unfamiliar ear, the apparent insolence of Israelis. On my first visit there, when I had the last echo of my good looks, I well remember the baffled Israeli boy who hit on me with the words 'I want – you want!' When I protested that I was married, he retorted '*He no here*! I want – you want!' Thankfully, my decrepit state means that this part-engaging, part-aggravating, carnal push-and-shove that is so much a part of Israeli life is now just a memory.

These days, I am not above playing the flaky old lady card to get through security sharpish. I always pack my Hebrew textbook at the top of my hand luggage, and when the fierce young operative seizes it and asks, 'Do you speak

Hebrew?' I answer, in my rustic child's voice '*Ani ohevet catulim veh kelevim!*' ('I love cats and dogs!') The effect is nothing short of miraculous, as the stern Semitic face breaks into a smile and a cry of whatever the Ivrit is for 'Here, come and listen to this freak, you won't believe it!' rings out across the El Al check-in area. Hebrew is difficult, beautiful, rebellious and, most importantly, the sensible choice for me, as I can't imagine a time when I won't want to keep going back to the land where they speak it. No matter how rude they are.

We got familiar with the Holocaust, very quickly, didn't we, as a world? Familiarity seems to have bred contempt, or at least weariness, in a very short time. Oh, Shoah – it's YOU again. Lighten up, can't you? Learn to take a joke. SHE'S IN THE ATTIC! Learn to be the punchline in six million fortune cookie philosophies: 'There are two ways to go to the gas chamber, free or not free' – Jean-Paul Sartre. There are death camp survivors still alive. Yet no one would dare write that about slavery.

'So there were all these women on the train – and basically, they were Jews.' The voice of a gay Polish hairdresser in the summer of 2013, as I write this book, reminds me of all the times before, when some half-wit chucked some throwaway remark into the innocent ether and rather than make me angry, just sealed my fate even tighter. 'But don't you ever think that if the Jews had never existed, there would be so much less trouble in the world?' a pretty teenage girl says to me soon after 9/11. Like a kaleidoscope of filth, it all comes back to me. Only one thing makes it bearable – that I have none of it in me. Here, at least, I am pure.

Tel Aviv, Summer 2013

When at home in England, I am a keen follower of the advice Winston Churchill once gave as he was trying to explain his success by applying Economy of Effort: 'Never stand up when you can sit down, and never sit down when you can lie down.' Later, a longer version would evolve from various grateful citizens: 'Never run when you can walk. Never walk when you can stand. Never stand when you can sit. Never sit when you can lie down. Never lay down when you can sleep.' But in Tel Aviv, I never sleep.

Instead, I walk. Up Allenby, down Jabotinsky, all along the esplanade from the old port to Jaffa. Through the White City of the clean Bauhaus dreamscape to Manta Ray, the most beautiful beachside restaurant in the world, with Karl. We practise our Hebrew; we shyly tell the sexy-dad waiter that we like the wine. He frowns. 'Where you from – Anglia? Your grammar is OK, but you sound too sweet. Say it angrier. NO, ANGRIER! Then you will sound Israeli.'

On Dizengoff Street I sit down and cry.

Why am I walking? What am I looking for? I am a fraud in this country of fanatical transparency and eye-watering candour. No one understands a word I say. No change there, then.

A man stops: '*Ma hasha'a?*'

I look at my watch: '*Chamesh.*'

'*Toda.*'

I get up, and walk on, looking for something.

References

Chapter 1

Asia Times Online. 'You love life, we love death'. *Asia Times*,March 24, 2004. http://www.atimes.com/ atimes/Front_Page/FC23Aa01.html.

Churchill, Winston. *A History of the English-Speaking Peoples: Vol 1: The Birth of Britain*. London: Cassell, 1956.

Daily Mail. 'Charles must go to Eton'. *Daily Mail*,January 28, 2013.

Davis Jr., Sammy. 'Is my mixed marriage messing up my kids?'. *Ebony*, October 1966.

Garrahan, Mathew. 'Will.i.am: the player'. *Financial Times*, August 31, 2012.

Gibson, Martin. 'No choice but to speak out – Israeli musician "a proud self-hating Jew"'. *Gisborne Herald*, January 23, 2009.

The Graham Norton Show. Series 11, Episode 11. June 22, 2012.

Hari, Johann. 'Agatha Christie – radical conservative thinker'. johannhari.com. Web. 4 October, 2003. http://johannhari.com/2003/10/04/agatha-christie-radical-conservative-thinker/.

Himmelfarb, Gertrude. *The People of the Book: Philosemitism in England, from Cromwell to Churchill*. New York: Encounter Books, 2011.

Hitchens, Christopher. *Hitch-22: A Memoir*. London: Atlantic Books, 2010.

Jen, Gish. *Mona in the Promised Land*. New York: Knopf, 1996.

Karpf, Anne. 'Anti-Semitism is at the limits of irony'. *Independent*, February 7, 2010.

Kashner, Sam and Nancy Schoenberger. *Furious Love: Elizabeth Taylor, Richard Burton: The Marriage of the Century*. London: JR Books, 2010.

Kelley, Kitty. *Elizabeth Taylor: The Last Star*.New York: Simon & Schuster, 2011.

McCarthy, Mary. *The Group*. London: Virago Press, 2009.

Murray, Charles. 'Jewish genius'. *Commentary*, January 4, 2007. http://www.commentarymagazine.com/article/jewish-genius/.

Primal Scream performing at Glastonbury Festival, 27 June, 2005.

Stilley, Margot. 'It's a strange time to be a Jew'. *The Sunday Times,* August 13, 2006. http://www.thesundaytimes.co.uk/sto/news/article160436.ece.

Chapter 2

Cutler, Adge. *Virtute et Industrial*. The Wurzels & Adge Cutler & The Wurzels. Sony/ATV, 1967.

McCarthy, Mary. *The Group*. London: Virago Press, 2009.

Schlesinger, Alex. 'Victorian jewry in Bristol'. n.d.

http://www.jewishgen.org/jcr-uk/Community/bri1/ History/.%5CVictorian.pdf.

Smith, Patti. *Seventh Heaven*. Philadelphia, Pa.: Telegraph Books, 1972.

Taylor, Elizabeth. *Elizabeth Takes Off: On Weight Gain, Weight Loss, Self-Image, and Self-Esteem*. New York: Putnam, 1987.

Yad Vashem. 'Overview: how vast was the crime'. n.d. http://www.yadvashem.org/yv/en/holocaust/about/ index.asp.

Chapter 3

New Musical Express. Job advertisement. July 1976.

Roth, Philip. *Portnoy's Complaint*. London: Vintage, 2005.

Sedaris, David. *Me Talk Pretty One Day*. New York: Little, Brown & Co., 2000.

Chapter 4

Bouchard, Albert and Patricia Lee Smith. *Career of Evil*. Secret Treaties. Sony/ATV, 1974.

Burchill, Julie. 'Well, whatever would Edvard Munch have said?'. *New Musical Express*, November 18 1978.

Coe, Jonathan. *The Rotters' Club*. London: Viking, 2001.

MacDermot, Galt, James Rado and Gerome Ragni. 'Easy to Be Hard'. From *Hair*, EMI Publishing Inc, 1969.

Shaar Murray, Charles. 'Give the anarchist a cigarette by Mick Farren'. *Independent*,December 7, 2001. http://archive.is/RewA2.

Thorn, Tracey. *Bedsit Disco Queen*. London: Virago, 2013).

Chapter 5

Landesman, Cosmo. *Starstruck: Fame, Failure, My Family and Me*. London: Macmillan, 2008.
Landesman, Jay. 'The designer rebel who slept in our spare room'. *Independent*, March 29, 1993. http://www.independent.co.uk/life-style/the-designer-rebel-who-slept-in-our-spare-room-julie-burchill-brought-white-bread-oldfashioned-values-and-angst-when-she-moved-in-with-her-inlaws-jay-landesman-remembers-1500674.html.
Round, Simon. 'Cosmo Landesman'. *The Jewish Chronicle*, October 17, 2008. http://www.thejc.com/arts/arts-interviews/cosmo-landesman.

Chapter 6

Burchill, Julie. 'Good, bad and ugly'. *Guardian*, November 29, 2003. http://www.theguardian.com/lifeand-style/2003/nov/29/weekend.julieburchill.
Fitzgerald, F. Scott and Edmund Wilson. *The Crack-Up*. New York: J. Laughlin, 1945.

Chapter 7

Baker, Mona and Gideon Toury. 'Correspondence with Gideon Toury'. June 8–11, 2002.

http://www.monabaker.com/pMachine/
more.php?id=531_0_1_12_M5.

Brown, Hannah. 'Behind "Unmasked," there is hope'.
Jerusalem Post, December 31, 2011.
http://www.jpost.com/Arts-and-Culture/Entertain-
ment/Behind-Unmasked-there-is-hope.

Coleman, Francesca. 'Lessons in hatred and abuse'. *The
Jewish Chronicle*, September 11, 2012.
http://www.thejc.com/comment-and-debate/com-
ment/78606/lessons-hatred-and-abuse.

The Commentator. 'Scottish hotel cancels Jewish event
after "threats"'. April 26, 2013.
http://www.thecommentator.com/article/3360/
scottish_hotel_cancels_jewish_event_after_threats.

Glassman, Jamie. 'Edinburgh comedians deny anti-Semitism. *The Times*, August 15, 2006.
http://www.theguardian.com/education/2008/nov/
14/oxford-students-bring-a-jew-party.

'Jane Elliott'. *Wikipedia*. n.d. http://en.wikipedia.org/
wiki/Jane_Elliott.

Julius, Anthony. *Trials of the Diaspora: A History of
Anti-Semitism in England*. Oxford: Oxford University
Press, 2010.

Levin, S. *Best Jewish Jokes*. London: Wolfe Pub., 1968.

Louvish, Simon. 'Nailing Spike'. *Guardian*, September 20,
2003. http://www.theguardian.com/books/2003/sep/
20/featuresreviews.guardianreview1.

Oz, Amos. *A Tale of Love and Darkness*. London: Vintage, 2005.

Paul, Jonny. 'British film director: rise in anti-Semitism
understandable'. *Jerusalem Post*, March 17, 2009.

http://www.jpost.com/International/British-film-director-Rise-in-anti-Semitism-understandable.

St Andrews Jewish Society Facebook Group. n.d. https://www.facebook.com/groups/2241105894/.

Chapter 8

'Archbishop's lecture – civil and religious law in England: a religious perspective'. *Archbishop's lecture*. February 7, 2008. http://rowanwilliams.archbishopofcanterbury.org/articles.php/1137/archbishops-lecture-civil-and-religious-law-in-england-a-religious-perspective.

The Avalon Project. *Hamas Covenant 1988*. August 18, 1988. http://avalon.law.yale.edu/20th_century/hamas.asp.

'British Chief Rabbi wants world parley to deal with intermarriage problem'. *The Global Jewish News Source*, February 7, 1968. http://www.jta.org/1968/02/07/archive/british-chief-rabbi-wants-world-parley-to-deal-with-intermarriage-problem.

Camber, Rebecca. '"No porn or prostitution": Islamic extremists set up Sharia law controlled zones in British cities'. *Daily Mail*,July 28, 2011.

Davies, Philip. 'Philip Davies MP: Consumers should have freedom of choice'. *Westminster Briefing*,February 24, 2012. http://www.westminster-briefing.com/news-detail/newsarticle/philip-davies-mp-consumers-should-have-freedom-of-choice/.

Forbes, Patrick. '*The Aristocrats*, Channel 4: "You don't

want to be the one who screws up"'. *Telegraph*,November 22, 2012.

Gilbert, Martin. *In Ishmael's House: A History of Jews in Muslim Lands*. New Haven, Conn.: Yale University Press, 2011.

Hirsi Ali, Ayaan. *Nomad: From Islam to America: A Personal Journey Through the Clash of Civilizations*. New York: Simon & Schuster, 2011.

Jones, Steve. "The John Maddox Lecture: Incest and Folk Dancing – Why Sex Survives'. Lecture, Hay Festival, May 28, 2011.

'Kaufman: Israel's Gaza "oppression" is like Iran'. *The Jewish Chronicle*, June 26, 2009.

Kelly, Tom. '"Bradford is very inbred": Muslim outrage as professor warns first-cousin marriages increase risk of birth defects'. *Daily Mail*, May 30, 2011.

Knight, India. 'Muslims are the new Jews'. *The Sunday Times*,October 15, 2006. http://www.thesundaytimes.co.uk/sto/news/Features/Focus/article158659.ece.

'Mosques to tackle grooming'. ITV News, June 28, 2013. http://www.itv.com/news/granada/2013-06-28/mosques-face-major-challenge-after-rigby-killing/.

O'Hagan, Andrew. 'Mel Gibson deserves pity, not pillory'. *Telegraph*, August 2, 2006. http://www.telegraph.co.uk/comment/personal-view/3626825/Mel-Gibson-deserves-pity-not-pillory.html.

Pappademas, Alex. 'Winona Forever'. *GQ*,January, 2011. http://www.gq.com/entertainment/celebrities/201101/winona-ryder-forever-black-swan-star-trek.

Pearson, Allison. 'Oxford grooming gang: We will regret

ignoring Asian thugs who target white girls'. *Telegraph*, May 15, 2013. http://www.telegraph.co.uk/news/uknews/crime/10060570/Oxford-grooming-gang-We-will-regret-ignoring-Asian-thugs-who-target-white-girls.html.

Peyer, Robin de. 'Legal action threatened over Banglatown ward scrappage'. *The Docklands & East London Advertiser*, November 19, 2012.

Raven, Charlotte. 'Know nothing about Afghanistan? Blame the death of the documentary'. *Guardian*, October 30, 2001. http://www.theguardian.com/world/2001/oct/30/afghanistan.comment.

Rayner, Gordon. 'White Muslim convert planned to steal bodyguard's gun and murder Prince Harry for having "blood on his hands"'. *Telegraph*,September 20, 2013. http://www.telegraph.co.uk/news/uknews/prince-harry/10324354/White-Muslim-convert-planned-to-steal-bodyguards-gun-and-murder-Prince-Harry-for-having-blood-on-his-hands.html.

Rich, Ben. 'We don't "marry out". We are made to'. *The Jewish Chronicle*, May 23, 2013. http://www.thejc.com/comment-and-debate/comment/107901/we-dont-marry-out-we-are-made.

Sacks, Jonathan. *Will We Have Jewish Grandchildren?: Jewish Continuity and How to Achieve it*. London: Vallentine Mitchell, 1994.

Tait, Nikki. 'Nightclub "was potential bomb target"'. *Financial Times*, March 23, 2006. http://www.ft.com/cms/s/0/c4654524-ba12-11da-9d02-0000779e2340.html#axzz2wSJtqT

The Times of Israel. 'Egyptian minister quotes Koran

verse on killing Jews'. *The Times of Israel*, April 5, 2013. http://www.timesofisrael.com/egyptian-minister-quotes-koran-verse-on-killing-jews/#ixzz2wRkKvjRQ.

Wynne-Jones, Jonathan. 'Archbishop says the Church will resist government moves on gay marriage'. *Telegraph*, February 26, 2011. http://www.telegraph.co.uk/news/religion/8349321/Archbishop-says-the-Church-will-resist-Government-moves-on-gay-marriage.html.

Chapter 9

Burchill, Julie. 'She's twigged: Macca has a thing for Jews'. *The Jewish Chronicle*, July 23, 2009. http://www.thejc.com/comment/comment/she's-twigged-macca-has-a-thing-jews.

Burchill, Julie. 'My quest for the one true faith'. *The Jewish Chronicle*, December 9, 2009. http://www.thejc.com/comment/columnists/24722/my-quest-one-true-faith.

Burchill, Julie. 'My loyalties won't fade away'. *The Jewish Chronicle*, December 22, 2010. http://www.thejc.com/comment-and-debate/columnists/42900/my-loyalties-wont-fade-away.

Butt, Riazat. 'Julie Burchill moves closer to Judaism'. *Guardian*,June 19, 2009. http://www.theguardian.com/world/2009/jun/19/julie-burchill-judaism-brighton-synagogue.

Fitzgerald, F. Scott and Edmund Wilson. *The Crack-Up*. New York: J. Laughlin, 1945.

'PCC backs Julie Burchill'. *The Jewish Chronicle*, Febru-

ary 18, 2010. http://www.thejc.com/news/uk-news/
28355/pcc-backs-julie-burchill.

Stalinsky, Steven. 'Dealing in death'. *National Review*,
May 24, 2004.

Tikvah Sarah, Elizabeth. 'Sukkot: a double legacy'. October 1, 2012. www.rabbiellisarah.com/sukkot-10th-
october-2012/.

Woolf, Cecily. 'Julie Burchill joins Brighton Shul'. *The
Jewish Chronicle*, June 18, 2009.
http://www.thejc.com/news/uk-news/julie-burchill-
joins-brighton-shul.

Chapter 10

Burchill, Julie. 'Bit of the other'. *Guardian*, October 23,
1999. http://www.theguardian.com/books/1999/oct/
23/fiction.reviews.

Burchill, Julie. 'Suffering under Uncle Sam'. *Guardian*,
September 16, 2000. http://www.theguardian.com/
lifeandstyle/2000/sep/16/weekend.julieburchill.

Evans, Peter and Ava Gardner. *Ava Gardner: The Secret
Conversations*. London: Simon & Schuster, 2013.

Grant, Linda. *When I Lived In Modern Times*. London:
Granta Books, 2000.

Kay, Richard. 'Richard Kay: No audience for Dame
Helen'. *Daily Mail*, April 2, 2013.

Landesman, Cosmo. 'When it comes to sexy Jews, I can't
compete with Schama'. *The Sunday Times*, August 18,
2013. http://www.thesundaytimes.co.uk/sto/com-
ment/columns/article1301188.ece.

Moran, Caitlin. *How to be a Woman*. London: Ebury Press, 2011.

Rashty, Sandy. 'Israeli shop "set to sue" protesters in Brighton'. *The Jewish Chronicle*, December 13, 2012. http://www.thejc.com/news/uk-news/94138/israeli-shop-set-sue'-protesters-brighton.

Acknowledgements

Toda raba to Levi Klein, who gave me the idea for this book; to Leah 'Honey B' Klein; Yael Breuer, for her astonishing patience with me while attempting to teach me the beautiful Hebrew language; Winston Pickett, for his understanding and empathy; Mark Wood for his encouragement; Caroline Gold for her passion; Dan One AND Dan Two; Ben, Simon, James, Jill, Monna, Hannah, Daniel and all the comrades on the Ecostream counterpicket. And of course, to the Jewish people themselves, for being every great thing they have been, are, and will be. L'chaim!

Subscribers

Unbound is a new kind of publishing house. Our books are funded directly by readers. This was a very popular idea during the late eighteenth and early nineteenth centuries. Now we have revived it for the internet age. It allows authors to write the books they really want to write and readers to support the writing they would most like to see published.

The names listed below are of readers who have pledged their support and made this book happen. If you'd like to join them, visit: www.unbound.co.uk.

Edward Allen

Jill Ashford

Rebekah Ashton

Laura Austin

Val Aviv

Alan Aziz

Steffen Bach

Sandra Barber

Sarah Barlow

David Berens

Eline Beun

Roger Bilboul

Jackie Bonham

Yael Breuer

Jeremy Brier

Deborah Brooks

Caraline Brown

Maria Brown

Catherine Burnett

Paul Burston

Jonathan Bush

Xander Cansell

Andrew Catlin

Kayo Chang

Ann Clare

Sandra Clifton

David Cohen

Matthew Coniam

D J Connell

David Conroy

Philippa Cooke

David Coppin

Amanda Craig

Sara Crammer

Julia Crouch

Sabina Crouch

Vickie Curtis

Neil Davenport

Graham Davies

Hazel Davis

Neil Denny

Housn D'espli

Trisha D'Hoker

Katie Downes

Yvonne Doyle

Rosemary Dun

Christine Dyer

Walter Eaves

Avril Egan

Ruth Eglash

Barbara Ellen

Gerald Epstein

Michael Ezra

Nigel Farndale

Alison Fisher

Caroline Foster

Tim Fountain

Harry Fox

Ilana Fox

Isobel Frankish

Seth Freedman

Sasha Frieze

Mark Futerman

Harriet Galgut

Jane Garcia

Garry Gelade

Shirley Geller

Carolyn Gill

Fabian Glagovsky

David Glass

Caroline Gold

Alice Goldie

Margot Gordon

Voula Grand

Ben Granger

Sarah Gredley

Dominic Green

Hazel Green

Paul Greenfield

Deborah Greenwood

Jane Griffiths

Stephanie Masha Gutmann

Jill Harman

David Harounoff

Nicky Harris

Adrian Hart

Caitlin Harvey
Naomi Hass
Louis Hemmings
Karl Henry
David Herman
Dennis Hobden
Jonathan Hoffman
Alex Hopkins
Keith Hotten
Michelle Huberman
Hilary Hughes
Ian Irvine
Michael Isaacs
Anthony Jacobs
Ruth Jacobs
Michèle Jaffé-Pearce
Peter James
Peter Jarrette
Kenneth Jassby
Jordan Jay Levy
Matt Judenfreund
Caroline Kaye and Kevin
    Gilligan
Howard Keeney
Judy Keiner
Alex Kemp
Dan Kieran
Gerry King
Gail Kinman
Hanja Kochansky
Philip Kremen

Nicholas Kryvicky
Miles La
Pierre L'Allier
Robin Landy
Karen Lang-Steel
Jimmy Leach
Anthony Lenaghan
Ruth Leveson
Ron Levi
Rosalind Levi
Ryan Levitt
Robert and Sally Levy
Markus Liebler
Marylou Linder
Richard Littlejohn
Candida Lycett Green
Maureen McKerrall
Tracy MacMillan-Cole
Nick Mailer
James Maker
Chris Mallows
Lucy Mallows
Steven Mann
Heather Marchant
Laura Marcus
Linda Marric
Ben Marshall
Gavin Martin
Brian May
Kate May
Jason Menayan

Neil Mendoza	Kate Ray
Michel and Susan Millodot	Barbara Raymond
Ryan Minchin	Christopher Raymond
John Mitchinson	Gillian Rhodes
Hugh Mooney	Chris Richards
Alie Moore	Robert Rinder
Caroline Moore	Carol Roberts
Michael Morgan	David Rose
Daniel Morgenstern	Daniel Rothenberg
Richard Murphy	Anthony Ruback
Paul Myers	Piers Russell-Cobb
Artur Neves	Gur Samuel
John Niven	Leyla Sanai
Brendan O'Neill	Jill Sanders
Fizzy Oppe	K Sansom
Alissa Ordabai	Luigi Santos-Hammarlund
Jim Owen	Shaheen Schelifer
Michael Paley	Rafi Schumacher
Jason Palmer	Toby Schumacher
Ian Payn	Habie Schwarz (me)
Jacqui Peleg	Geoff Segar
Mark Persad	Jonathan & Fiona Seitler
Sandra Phillips	David Sherman
Julie Pinkham	Ivan Silverstein
Justin Pollard	David Silverston
John Porter	Jon Simmons
Gail Potts	Susannah Simon
Walter Pretorius	Jonathan Simpson
Mariano Raigón	Catriona Smith
Michele Rajput	Helen Smith
Rose Ratcliffe	Mark Solomons

Maurice Solovitz
Melanie Spencer
Eva Speter
Alex Stafford
Matthew Starr
Alex Stein
Anna Steiner
Cindy Stern
Peter Stokes
Richard Stoliar
Sian Sturgis
Mitchell Symons
Dror Tankus
Sara Teal
Andrew Tibber
Karen Tobias-Green
Pieter Uys
Mark Walklett
Marc Walters
Robin Watt
Kate Watt Watt
Theodora Wayte

Sian Webley
Stephen West
Francis Wheen
Stephen White
Cassandra Wilkinson
Jo Willcox
Sarah Williams
Astrid Williamson
Jo Wilson
Philip Witriol
Natascha Wolf
Louise Wolfson
David Wolfson QC
Mark Wood
David Woolfson
Shivaun Woolfson
Alison Young
Samantha Zahringer
Liz Zeid
Zionist Federation UK
Debi Zylbermann

Credits